Alphabet Animals

PATTERNS FOR APPLIQUÉ

■ ■ ■

Alphabet Animals

PATTERNS FOR APPLIQUÉ

■ ■ ■

Paula Latos Valier

Sterling Publishing Co., Inc.   New York

Library of Congress Cataloging-in-Publication Data
Valier, Paula Latos.
    Alphabet animals.

    Originally published: Crafty animals. Australia :
Ellsyd Press, 1987.
    1. Appliqué—Patterns.   2. Decoration and ornament—
Animal forms.   I. Title
TT779.V35   1989   746.44'5041   88-35628
ISBN 0-8069-6905-9

1   3   5   7   9   10   8   6   4   2

Published in 1989 by Sterling Publishing Co., Inc.
Two Park Avenue, New York, N.Y. 10016
First published in 1987 in Australia copyright
text © Ellsyd Press Pty Ltd, copyright designs
© Paula Latos Valier under the title, "Crafty Animals"
Distributed in Canada by Oak Tree Press Ltd.
c/o Canadian Manda Group, P.O. Box 920, Station U
Toronto, Ontario, Canada M8Z 5P9
Manufactured in the United States of America
All rights reserved

Sterling ISBN 0-8069-6905-9   Paper

Design by John Byrne
Typeset by Love Computer Typesetting, Sydney

Produced by Mandarin Offset
Printed and bound in Hong Kong

Introduction

All the designs in this book are based on a simple applique method which involves layering the cut out shapes in order to form pictures. They have been sewn in felt but can be made in a variety of fabrics and materials, from colored paper to scraps of cloth. The designs can be embellished or simplified as you please and will prove a source of fun for children and adults alike.

Parents, for example, can use them to make quilts, covers or wall hangings for their children's rooms, or they can sew individual designs onto T-shirts or sweatshirts to give a new lease of life to old items or customize new ones.

As most of the pictures are constructed of simple shapes, all of which are provided at the back of the book, young children can learn to recognize not only the letters of the alphabet and specific animals but also how shapes in combination form pictures. Learning to see pictures can be lots of fun. Children can also cut out the shapes to make collages. Crayons, scissors, glue, fabric or colored paper are all they need to get started.

As you can see, this book has many uses — we have mentioned only a few. Don't forget your imagination!

A a
Alligator

B b
Beaver

C c
Cockatoo

D d

Dog

E e
Elephant

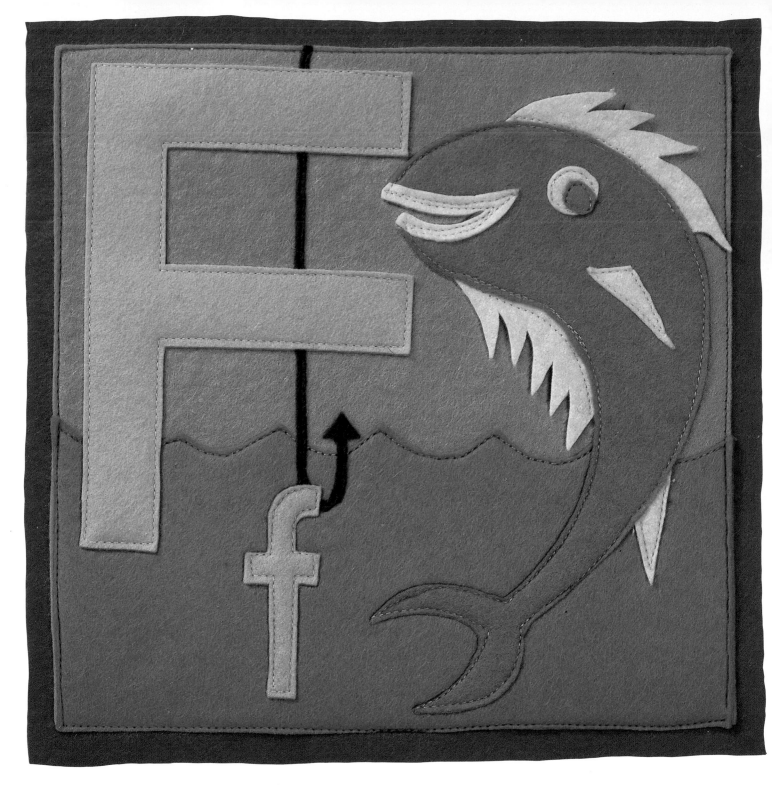

F f
Fish

G g
Goose

H h
Horse

I i

Iguana

J j
Jellyfish

Kk

Koala

L l
Lion

M m
Mouse

N n

Nest

O o
Owl

P p
Penguin

Q q
Quail

R r
Rabbit

S s
Seal

T t
Turtle

U u
Unicorn

V v

Vulture

W w
Whale

Xx
Mystery Animal

Y y

Yak

Z z
Zebra

Applique is a simple process of layering one piece of fabric on top of another. Nothing can be simpler.

If you do a bit of sewing now and then, you will probably find all you need in your sewing basket. The following are the main requirements.

Scissors

The basis of all applique is cutting out shapes in fabric. Good sharp dressmaker's shears should therefore be used. For fine work, you may use fine pointed embroidery scissors. Pinking shears give a zigzag edge useful for special effects and for adding a decorative note to frayless fabrics such as felt, suede and leather.

Pattern paper

If you choose to trace the shapes at the back of the book, a variety of papers can be used. The best is tracing paper, available from art supply stores, but you may find that your kitchen cupboards will provide suitable tracing paper if you handle it carefully. Waxed or unwaxed lunch paper is transparent enough to be used for tracing and it is much less expensive. Butcher's paper is also recommended as it is strong, though transparent. If the paper is not large enough for your grid, you can join it with invisible tape.

Fabrics

Many fabrics are appropriate for applique and often scraps and remnants from your sewing basket are adequate. If you choose to use the designs on clothing or household items which will be laundered frequently, it is best to use washable fabrics such as cotton, linen or blends.

Fabric glue

If you choose not to stitch the shapes, the pictures can be constructed quickly and simply by using fabric glue. A range of fabric glues is available from most craft supply shops. This is also a good way of getting children involved in the construction of pictures and will help them learn to use simple tools like scissors and glue. Make sure you check the label to ensure that the glue is suitable for all fabrics and is also water-resistant.

Sewing machine

All domestic sewing machines are basically the same and will machine both straight and zig-zag stitches. However, some machines incorporate special functions, such as embroidery stitches, which can be useful and decorative.

Threads

To stitch an applique in place, any fine mercerized cotton thread or polyester thread may be used. Mercerised cotton has been specially treated for shrinkage and has added strength. Polyester thread is the better choice if the article is to be laundered often as it has the ability to stretch and recover. Consider how the finished piece will be laundered before buying cotton thread as this may shrink and cause unwanted puckers in the fabric.

How to Get the Best Results

The following are some useful hints which apply to all the designs.

Layering

When two or more pieces are appliqued, it is important to plan how they will fit together. Shapes that appear behind others must be properly positioned and sewn first. The layers are then built upwards. Because of this layering order, you cannot sew all the applique sections in place at one time. This is not as important for collage (using glue) as it is for applique (using stitching).

The simplest way to make the pictures work, with the least amount of frustration, is to cut out all the pieces in your chosen material before beginning to assemble them. Then pin them in position. This will allow you to make minor adjustments in the placement of details such as eyes, teeth, beaks and ears. Keep in mind, however, that it is easier to put the details of eyes, ears and noses onto the body shape before putting the larger piece on to your background. Sometimes the slight shift in position or angle will create a different personality for the animal. You may wish to experiment with this and create your own expressions!

Tracing and cutting

All the pattern pieces at the back of the book represent the actual shape in the finished design. Allowance has not been made for folding under edges for lighter weight fabrics. If you choose fabrics which require a folded hem around the border to keep them from fraying, you must allow a little extra fabric around each pattern piece when cutting out the shapes. Five or six millimetres will do.

If, however, you intend to use a zigzag stitch to avoid fraying and to create a strong graphic line in the finished picture, you will not need this extra margin of fabric.

There are several ways you can work from the pattern pieces you have traced and cut. They can be put on top of the surface of the cloth you wish to cut and traced in soft pencil, tailor's chalk or even felt pen provided you cut carefully so your tracing line does not show. Experienced sewers might be able to simply cut around the pattern pieces without drawing first. But do make sure you pin your pattern

carefully so that it does not shift as you cut.

The process of tracing on paper and then onto fabric will mean that the outline of the pattern piece will be slightly larger than the original in the book. To compensate for this, cut the fabric on the inside of your tracing line rather than on the outside. This will also eliminate any telltale tracing marks so that all your fabric pieces will be clean-edged and ready to sew.

Stitching

The pictures illustrated in the front of the book have all been sewn with a straight running stitch, the simplest of all machine stitching. This method has been used so you can clearly see where the stitching falls. In most cases, the color of the thread has been chosen to match the color of the applique piece. You may wish to experiment with contrasting colors to highlight your pictures.

If you wish to use a zigzag stitch, it is a good idea to test the stitch on scraps similar to your applique and garment fabrics. Start machining along the straightest edge of your applique shape, zigzagging over the raw edges. Carefully guide the applique, sewing a little at a time. When the sewing is complete, leave long ends of the thread and tie them at the back.

It is always best to proceed slowly regardless of which stitch you are using and to feed the fabric gently and evenly under the foot of your machine. Take care not to stretch the fabric so that you don't get gathers and puckers on outside curves. In these cases, you will need to ease your fabric gently under the foot of the machine. If you push too quickly, the fabric will buckle and gather.

If you wish to sew the animal shapes directly onto clothes or household items, without their background patches, the principles remain the same. Construct the smaller elements first (such as details of eyes, teeth, etc.) before mounting the whole design on your garment.

Do keep in mind, however, that sewing the animal shapes and letters directly onto large pieces of fabric such as tablecloths or bedspreads, will require more skill and patience. If, instead, they are mounted on a background patch, as shown in all the illustrations, you simply need to sew four straight lines to attach the patch.

Texture

Texture can be highlighted by the type of fabric, the embroidery details or the trimmings, such as beads, pompoms or braid, employed in the design. For example, the zebra stripes can be done in decorative stitching rather than with pieces of cloth. Or you may choose to use striped fabric. You may wish to create a whole range of textures, a snake skin patterned fabric for the iguana or fake fur for the lion or a pompom for the rabbit's tail.

Enlarging the designs

If you want to enlarge any of the designs to make a wall hanging, for example, simply make a grid on a piece of tracing paper and lay it on top of the line drawing at the back of the book. Trace the drawing onto your grid. You can then blow up the drawing, square by square, to the desired size by simply enlarging the grid and faithfully copying the shapes which appear in each square of the grid. This is a handy way of enlarging anything and, though it might take a bit of practice at first, it is a very simple procedure.

If you find this a daunting task, your local instant printer will be able to enlarge or reduce your chosen design to the required size.

The Designs

The following are step-by-step instructions to all the designs in the book but, first, some general instructions which apply to each applique.

First trace and cut out all the shapes at the back of the book for the picture you wish to construct. (It is best not to cut out the book itself as the pages are printed back to back.) Take your cut out paper shapes and place them right side up on the fabric of your choice. Experienced sewers may be able to simply pin them in place and cut around the pattern pieces but it is more accurate to trace the pattern pieces with pencil or chalk onto the fabric, then to remove the pattern piece and cut along the traced lines. Take care to cut just inside the lines so that no telltale tracing marks show up on your finished picture.

Once all the pieces are cut out, it is time to begin the assembly which involves layering and overlapping the cloth pieces. Refer to the color reproductions at the front of the book for guidance.

If you wish to construct a colored frame around your applique, simply mount it on a larger square of cloth. The outer edge of the frame is 260 mm (10.5 in) square. This is the standard patchwork size which has been used throughout the book. The inside background patch is 240 mm (9.5 in) square.

Alligator

1 Begin by placing the alligator's body onto the background square (see illustration). Adjust its position carefully and temporarily pin it to keep it in place, leaving the head unpinned for now.

2 Take the small piece for the alligator's tongue and, lifting the head, slip the tongue behind the mouth opening. On top of the tongue place the second layer and the jagged teeth. Then lay the head back on top of these two layers and pin snugly in place. You may need to shift them slightly so that they are in exactly the right position inside the aligators jaws.

3 At this point, you can sew just along the edge of the alligator's mouth from the nose to the lower jaw. This will keep the tongue and teeth pieces in place. Then sew the jagged edge of the teeth and the tongue.

4 Pin the two crescent-shaped eyelids in position. Next sew the pupil over the large eye of the alligator and place the eye beneath the right eyelid. Stitch the eyelids, then the eye.

5 You can now sew from the nose, along the top edge of the face, forehead and back of the head. Add the two triangular nostril holes and your face is complete.

6 Next take the two pieces for the right and left legs and pin and stitch them in place.

7 Now construct the ball. Take the round cloth shape and center the letter 'a' on it. Pin and sew. Position the ball so the chin of the alligator just overlaps the top of the ball and about a quarter of the ball extends over the alligator's belly. Pin in place and sew the ball onto the patch. Now you can sew the bottom edge of the alligator's chin so that it just overlaps the top edge of the ball. Extend your stitching so that you create the lower jaw line.

8 Sew around the outer edge of the alligator's body, along the length of the tail and spiny back. If you sew a straight line under the jagged edge it creates a nice effect.

9 Next pin the hands on, making sure that the claws of the right hand overlap the ball's right edge and the left claws overlap the left edge of the ball. Stitch down.

10 Lastly, sew the 'A' in place.

Beaver

1 Place the body shape in a diagonal position with the head towards the lower left corner. Position the feet on top of the ends of the legs and pin in place. Do the same with the right hand.

2 Next take the piece for the tail and sew the spine of the tail in place. Position the tail under the body edge and pin in place.

3 At this point you will be able to tell if any of the pieces need to be slightly adjusted for position. When you are happy that everything fits in place, stitch around the body, then around the hands, feet and tail, leaving a small opening at the mouth to insert the teeth. Using a different shade of thread, sew the shape of the fingers and toes to make the webbed feet.

4 Now it's time to put the eye, nose and small freckles at the base of the whiskers onto the beaver. It is probably easier to stitch the freckles in place by hand as they are very small. Also, stitch a curved line which goes from the teeth and under the eye to create a smiling mouth.

5 Place the branch at the bottom of the picture so that it appears to be held by the mouth of the beaver. Pin and sew. The leaves can be attached to the edge of the twigs by a single line of stitching down the center of each leaf.

6 With lines of stitching, make whiskers which protrude from the freckles. You may need to go over the stitched lines several times to create thick enough lines.

7 Sew the letters in place.

8 Finally, add the air bubbles to create an underwater effect.

Cockatoo

1 Place the body shape of the cockatoo just to the right of the middle line of the background patch and pin in position leaving the top of the head loose.

2 Insert the crest under the feathered edge of the top of the cockatoo's head. It should just fit inside the top and right edges of the corner of your patch.

3 Pin the pieces for the beak and the eye in place.

4 Place the 'c' so that it appears to be held by the beak.

5 Make minor adjustments to positioning and stitch the pieces in place beginning with the crest, leaving the feathered edge of the far left side of the crest unattached for the moment. Then sew the body, the 'c', the beak and, finally, the eye.

6 To give the cockatoo a little detail, stitch the three small tail feathers in place at the center bottom of the tail.

7 Position the 'C' on the upper left of the patch, pin and sew. Now you can sew the far left side of the feathered edge of the crest over the top edge of the letter 'C'.

8 Place the branch at the bottom of the picture (see illustration) and stitch. Add the leaves and feet and stitch in place.

Dog

1 First construct the dog. Position the markings for the tail, foreleg, head and spots and stitch down. Do the same for the eye, the nose and the dog collar.

2 Position the finished dog on the left side of the patch and pin in place. Before sewing the outside edge of the dog on to the patch, lift the head and place the tongue in position underneath the open mouth. Sew all pieces, except the tail, in place.

3 Position and sew the 'D' and, when complete, stitch down the tail so that it overlaps the bottom of the 'D'.

4 Place the 'd' in the lower right corner. Pin and sew.

Elephant

1 Pin the shape of the elephant at a slight angle on the right side of your patch (see illustration).

2 On the right side of the head place the piece for the ear and at the bottom corner, the piece for the tail.

3 Stitch around the edge of the entire elephant, leaving only the tip of the mouth free.

4 Place the right arm in position. Pin and sew.

5 Now pin the four pads for the hands and feet and the tip of the trunk in place and sew.

6 Construct the eye and sew in place.

7 Take the shape for the open mouth and pin in place but do not sew.

8 Now sew the 'e' onto the ball and place so that it balances on the top of the elephant's head and overlaps the tip of the trunk. Pin and sew.

9 Finally, position the 'E' (see illustration) and stitch down. Attach the piece for the open mouth so that it overlaps the edge of the 'E'.

Fish

1 Place the piece with the wavy edge for the water at the bottom of the background patch. Pin and sew.

2 Construct the fish by attaching the lips, the eye and the small side fin. Pin these in place and sew onto the body of the fish.

3 Position the fish on the right side of the background patch and pin in place so that the tail ends almost at the bottom centre of the picture (see illustration). Now place the three remaining fin pieces under the back and belly of the body and sew in place.

4 Position the fishing line at the top edge of the patch so that the hook appears just over the surface of the water and stitch.

5 Sew down the 'f' so that it appears to be hooked on

the fish hook.

6 Lastly, attach the 'F'.

Goose

1 Pin the shape for the grass at the bottom of the background patch. Stitch in place.

2 Position the egg shape at the bottom right corner of the grass and sew.

3 Stitch down the 'g' in the bottom left corner.

4 Center the body of the goose on the patch and pin. Position the two webbed feet under the goose, then sew around the edge of the body. This will hold the legs in place.

5 Sew the legs and feet, using stitching to create the effect of webbed feet.

6 Attach the beak and the eye and sew in place.

7 You can now create the wing and tail feathers with lines of stitching.

8 Lastly, sew the 'G' in place.

Horse

1 Place the eye, nostril and teeth in position and stitch down. You can use stitching to highlight the teeth.

2 Sew the two hooves to the ends of the legs.

3 Position the constructed horse (see illustration) and pin in place. Sew around the head and body, using stitching to create the lower jaw and to define the right leg.

4 Position the forelock on the forehead of the horse and the mane on the neck. Stitch down.

5 Now construct the bridle and reins by placing the four pieces — as shown in the illustration — over the nose and along the side of the horse's head. Position the 'H', wrapping the reins around the letter, and stitch all in place.

6 Finally, position the 'h' in the lower right corner and stitch down.

Iguana

1 Place the piece for the earth at the bottom of the background patch and sew.

2 Position the body shape of the iguana on the center of your patch with its head to the top right hand corner. Stitch around the outside edge of the body, leaving the mouth opening unattached so you can slip the tongue behind the open mouth. Sew the tongue and mouth.

3 You can now create the shape of the thigh and shoulder with a line of stitching.

4 Next, position the jagged spine flush against the edge of the back starting at the top of the head and running it along the top edge of the tail. Sew in place, proceeding slowly to prevent the narrow spine from slipping out of position.

5 Sew the eye and pupil in place.

6 Now stitch the letters in place so that the 'I' overlaps the tail of the iguana and the 'i' floats in the sky.

Jellyfish

1 Sew the scalloped edge of the sky at the top of the background fabric piece.

2 Sew the small parachute shape of the body of the jellyfish onto the larger parachute shape. Pin on the patch so that it appears to be just under the surface of the water (see illustration).

3 Take the piece with the seven tendrils and pin in place under the bottom edge of the parachute shape, leaving the tendrils themselves unattached.

4 Next, position the three long arms of the jellyfish as illustrated. Pin in place and arrange the tendrils so that they weave in and out of the longer arms. Don't sew at this stage. Refer to the color illustration for correct positioning throughout all these steps.

5 Place the 'J' just to the left of the parachute shape and allow the second and fourth tendril to overlap it.

6 When you are pleased with the floating look of the jellyfish, stitch down the 'J', then the tendrils and arms in whichever order you please.

7 Now stitch the parachute-shaped body.

8 Finally, pin and stitch the 'j' in place.

Koala

1 Pin the body shape of the koala on the left side of the patch, placing the lighter coloured fabric for the chest and belly under the arm and the leg. Sew all around the body shape but leave the hand and foot unattached.

2 Pin the eyes, nose, nostrils and chin tuft in place, making sure the tuft is tucked under the lower edge of the nose, then stitch down. Place the ear tufts just inside the ears and stitch.

3 Position the two pieces for the branch on either side of the chin tuft and stitch in place. Sew the leaves at the ends of the twigs, using a single line of stitching down the spine of each leaf.

4 Position the 'K' and sew in place, making sure that the hand and foot overlap the 'K'.

5 Sew the hand and the foot in place and add the claws at the very end.

6 Sew 'k' in position.

Lion

1 Centre the large body shape of the lion on your background patch. Pin in place, then stitch along the outer edge and along the fingers of the two front paws.

2 Place the mane over the body and stitch down.

3 Pin the single shape for the nose and mouth so that it touches the two curves at the inside edge of the mane. You can highlight the nostrils by putting a lighter coloured fabric behind the open nostril holes. Stitch down.

4 Construct the eyes and position them slightly slanted just under the ear holes. Stitch in place.

5 Pin the two crescent shapes for the ears so that they overlap the mane and sew in place.

6 Center the beard below the mouth and stitch down.

7 Use a single line of stitching from the corner of the eye to the edge of the nose to create the bridge of the nose.

8 Lines of stitching can also be used to create the whiskers.

9 Add the tuft of the tail so that it just touches the top edge of the patch.

10 Sew the letters in place (see illustration).

Mouse

1 Pin the shape of the mouse on the diagonal so that the nose is in the lower left corner and the tail points to the upper right corner (see illustration). Stitch around the outside edge, leaving the ears unattached and using your stitching to define the shape of the right arm, the right leg, the paws, the belly and the top of the head.

2 Add the eye and nose and stitch in place.

3 Create whiskers with stitching on either side of the nose.

4 Place the 'M' in the top left corner of the patch so that the left ear overlaps the bottom left of the 'M' and stitch down. Place the two pieces for the inner and outer right ear overlapping the 'M'. Stitch in place.

5 Stitch the 'm' in the bottom right corner.

Nest

1 First construct the cracked egg with the chick inside. To do this, sew the eye and beak in place and position the head on top of the egg. Over the neck of the chick place the cracked half of the egg so that the head appears to be peeping out of the shell. Stitch the head and cracked egg in place.

2 Construct the nest by overlapping the two pieces which make the nest (see illustration). Slip the eggs under the jagged inside edge of the top piece of the nest so that all three eggs can be seen and the cracked egg is on top. Once these are positioned, attach the eggs to the bottom piece of the nest. Then stitch down the top piece of the nest so that the eggs appear to be sitting inside the nest.

3 Position the branch (see illustration). Place the nest on the patch so that it overlaps the center limb of the branch, pin but do not sew.

4 Position the 'N' in the top left corner of the patch, allowing the top twigs to poke through the letter (see illustration).

5 Adjust the position of all the elements of the design and pin in place. Then begin stitching in the following order: the bottom section of the branch, the nest itself, the 'N' and, lastly, the topmost twigs which extend over the 'N'.

6 Now attach the leaves and sew a single line to create the spine of each leaf.

7 Sew the 'n' in place in the upper right corner.

Owl

We have not included a pattern piece for the hillside in this picture but it is easy to make one. Using a ruler, draw an open-topped rectangle approximately 240 mm (9.5 in) wide and 135 mm (5.3 in) high on your tracing paper. Close up the open top by drawing a wavy line, as in the illustration, to represent the hillside.

1 Position the hillside shape to the bottom of the patch and stitch down.

2 Pin the facial features to the body shape of the owl, starting with the heart-shaped face, then the facial outline shape, the eyes and the beak. Sew all facial features in place.

3 Add the small dots on either side of the chest. You may need to stitch these by hand as they are very small.

4 Add the left wing to the shoulder of the owl and set the constructed owl aside.

5 Position the tail of the owl so that its bottom edge is flush with the bottom edge of the background and place the constructed body on top (see illustration). Position the right wing so that it goes from the right shoulder to the bottom edge of the patch, along the right edge of the tail.

6 When the placement is correct, sew, leaving the thighs unattached so that the feet can be inserted later.

7 Add the branch at the bottom left of the patch. Pin, but don't sew until you have positioned the feet so that the claws appear to hold the branch. Sew the branch and the feet, making sure you stitch down the thighs.

8 Place the 'O' in the top right corner of the patch so that it overlaps the shoulder of the owl.

9 The 'o' fits in the lower right corner.

10 Lastly, attach the crescent-shaped moon.

Penguin

1 Construct the eye of the penguin and stitch to the head.

2 Position the head on top of the body shape and stitch down.

3 Add the colored tips to the penguin's flippers and stitch in place.

4 Pin the shape for the back and tail to the penguin's body and stitch down.

5 Position the flippers on either side of the body and place feet under the two little bumps at the bottom of the penguin's body. You can create the webbed feet by stitching between the toes of the penguin.

6 When all the elements are positioned to your satisfaction, stitch them in place, leaving the bill of the penguin free until you insert the small fish. Then stitch the bill and fish.

7 Pin the letters in place and stitch down (see illustration).

Quail

1 First construct the body and head of the quail. Position the wing and back shape, then stitch down. Add the special markings which consist of stripes, squares and rectangles. (We have not included pattern pieces because these shapes are so simple. You may choose to make your own markings with embroidery stitches.) Next attach the eye and the bill of the quail. The body of the bird is now complete.

2 Position the quail in the center of your patch and pin, slipping the feet under the belly of the bird. Stitch around the body and feet.

3 Pin the letters in place as illustrated and stitch.

Rabbit

1 Pin the eye, nose and right inner ear to the head and stitch down.

2 Place the piece for the rabbit's chest and under belly beneath the rabbit's chin and front leg (refer to the white section in the illustration), pin and stitch.

3 You can emphasize the furlike quality by jagged stitching around the arm, leg and chin (see illustration).

4 Pin the constructed rabbit on the center of the patch. Slip the tail in position and pin down. Place the carrot under the right paw of the rabbit and add the green top.

5 When all elements are positioned carefully, stitch down, beginning with the carrot and continuing around the entire edge of the rabbit. Create the fingers and toes, the rabbit's smiling face, the whiskers and the markings on the carrot with lines of stitching.

6 Finally, pin and sew the letters in place (see illustration).

Seal

1 Attach the eye to the head of the seal and place the body shape on the bottom of the patch so that there is space to fit the ball on top of the nose. Pin in position but do not stitch.

2 Pin the 's' to the ball and stitch. Place in position on the top of the nose of the seal so that it appears to balance.

3 Position the 'S' on the left side of the patch and bring the seal's tail through the bottom curve of the 'S' so that it overlaps. Pin in place.

4 After making any minor adjustments, stitch all elements in place, beginning with the ball and continuing on to the body of the seal. Sew the tail in place before completing the lower half of the 'S'.

5 Add the small black nose of the seal so that it overlaps the lower edge of the ball. As it is small it is probably easiest to sew by hand.

6 You can create whiskers, flippers and the detail on the tail with lines of stitching.

Turtle

1 Place the oval of the turtle's back on the body shape and stitch down.

2 Construct the eye of the turtle and stitch in place.

3 Position the constructed turtle at the bottom left of your patch and pin.

4 Position the two seaweed pieces in the bottom corners (see illustration), making sure that the left leg of the turtle overlaps the seaweed. Pin in place.

5 Stitch the seaweed and the turtle in place, leaving the tip of the top flipper unattached so that it can overlap the 'T'.

6 Position the 'T' in the top left corner so that it overlaps the back of the turtle. Pin and stitch in place. Attach the turtle's top left flipper on top of the 'T'.

7 Stitch down the 't' at the top right of the patch.

8 Sew the bubbles in place.

Unicorn

1 Sew the shape for the grass flush to the bottom right corner of your patch.

2 Position the eye, the earhole and the nose to the head of the unicorn and stitch down.

3 Position the body shape (see illustration), pin and sew in place.

4 Pin and stitch the mane and horn of the unicorn in position.

5 You can create the lower jaw, the smiling mouth and the spiral effect of the horn with stitching.

6 Position the letters on the left side of the patch (see illustration), pin and sew.

Vulture

1 First construct the body of the vulture by positioning the wing and shoulder shapes correctly (see illustration). Pin and sew.

2 Pin the constructed body to the center of the patch.

3 Centre the shape for the mountain top at the bottom of the patch so that it is directly under the belly of the vulture. Pin in position but do not sew until the feet are correctly placed.

4 Stitch down the mountain top, then the feet and, finally, the body of the vulture.

5 Use stitching to create the wing and tail feathers.

6 Add the head so that it slightly overlaps the neck of the vulture. Pin and sew.

7 Sew the eye and nostril in place.

8 Use stitching to create the wrinkles at the base of the neck and around the eye. A line of stitching will also define the beak.

9 Place letters in position as illustrated and stitch down.

Whale

We have not included a pattern piece for the water in this picture but it is easy to make one. Using a ruler, draw a rectangle approximately 240 mm (9.5 in) wide and 135 mm (5.3 in) high, leaving the top end open. Close up the top end by drawing in a scalloped line, as in the illustration, to represent the waves.

1 Place the wavy piece for the water at the bottom of the patch and stitch down.
2 Sew the eye and the small shape for the blow hole in position.
3 Pin the whale to the bottom center of the patch. You may have to make minor adjustments in order to fit both the tail and the nose of the whale within the water. Slip in the teeth so that their jagged edge shows above the lower jaw and pin in position.
4 When you are happy with the positioning of the various components, stitch in place.
5 If you wish, sew a second line of stitching along the edge of the teeth.
6 Position the three small pieces which represent the splash from the blow hole just above the blow hole opening and stitch in place.
7 Add the bubbles (see illustration).
8 Position both letters as in the illustration, pin and stitch.

Mystery Animal

1 Construct the eyes by first placing the 'Xs' over the large circles, then add the eyeballs. Position on the head of the animal and stitch down.
2 Position the nose so that it touches the top of the head (see illustration), add the two circles for the nostrils and stitch down.
3 Place the smiling mouth under the nose and pin the teeth in position (see illustration). Stitch mouth and teeth in place.
4 Place the right arm on the right side of the body and stitch.
5 Position the constructed animal on the right side of the patch and stitch down.
6 Pin the letters to the left side of the patch so that the top of the 'X' overlaps the left arm of the animal (see illustration). Stitch down.
7 Position the left hand of the animal so that it appears to be holding the top of the 'X' and stitch in place.
8 Add the claws to the hands and feet.

Yak

1 First construct the head of the yak by pinning in place the muzzle, the nostrils, the eyes and the hair on top of the head. Stitch down.
2 Place the constructed head on the right side of the body shape (the side with the larger hump). When satisfied with its position, stitch down.
3 Position the constructed body in the centre of the patch. Under the ragged lower edge, insert the four legs (as illustrated). Pin and stitch down the body and legs.
4 To the base of the legs sew the four hooves.
5 Place the horns in position and stitch down.
6 Position the letters and stitch (see illustration).

Zebra

This is the most detailed and difficult of all the pictures but, by now, you will be an expert so have fun!

We have not included a pattern for the grass in this picture but it is easy to make one. Using a ruler, draw a rectangle approximately 240 mm (9.5 in) wide, 85 mm (3.3 in) high on the left side and 65 mm (2.5 in) high on the right, leaving the top end open. Now, using the illustration as a guide, create the grass by closing up the open end with an uneven jagged line. The grass should slope down towards the bottom of the zebra's nose and up again to meet the other side (see illustration).

1 First construct the zebra. Remember that the zebra's stripes are irregular and no two zebras look alike, so don't worry about following the striped pieces too closely. Once you have pinned all the stripes in place (they are numbered from left to right on the pattern pieces at the back of the book), including the larger shape for the muzzle, make any minor adjustments and then stitch them down, leaving the tail for later.
2 Add the details for the nostril, the eye and the tips of the ears.
3 Position the zebra, then the shape for the grass, making sure the grass overlaps the bottom edge of the zebra and is flush with the bottom of the patch. Pin in place. Then slip the mane in at the top of the head and proceed to stitch all elements in place.
4 Pin and stitch down the letters (see illustration).
5 Place the piece for the tail in position so that it overlaps the bottom part of the 'Z'.
6 Position the stripes on the tail and the tip of the tail. Stitch all in place.

Handy hints

- Check fabrics and threads for color fastness before using them.

- Press all fabrics to remove wrinkles or creases before cutting them.

- Some fabrics press better with a pressing cloth.

- Pressing your work as you proceed through the steps makes it easier to sew, especially when edges are folded under.

- Check your layering order before stitching down the shapes and always pin them in place before sewing.

- Pull machine sewing thread ends to the back of your work, when finished, and tie them off before cutting.

- If you have used buttons, beads or similar features, press carefully around them.

Eyelid

Eye

Eye

Eyelid

Nostril

Nostril

Tongue

Hand

Right Leg

Right
Arm

Left Leg

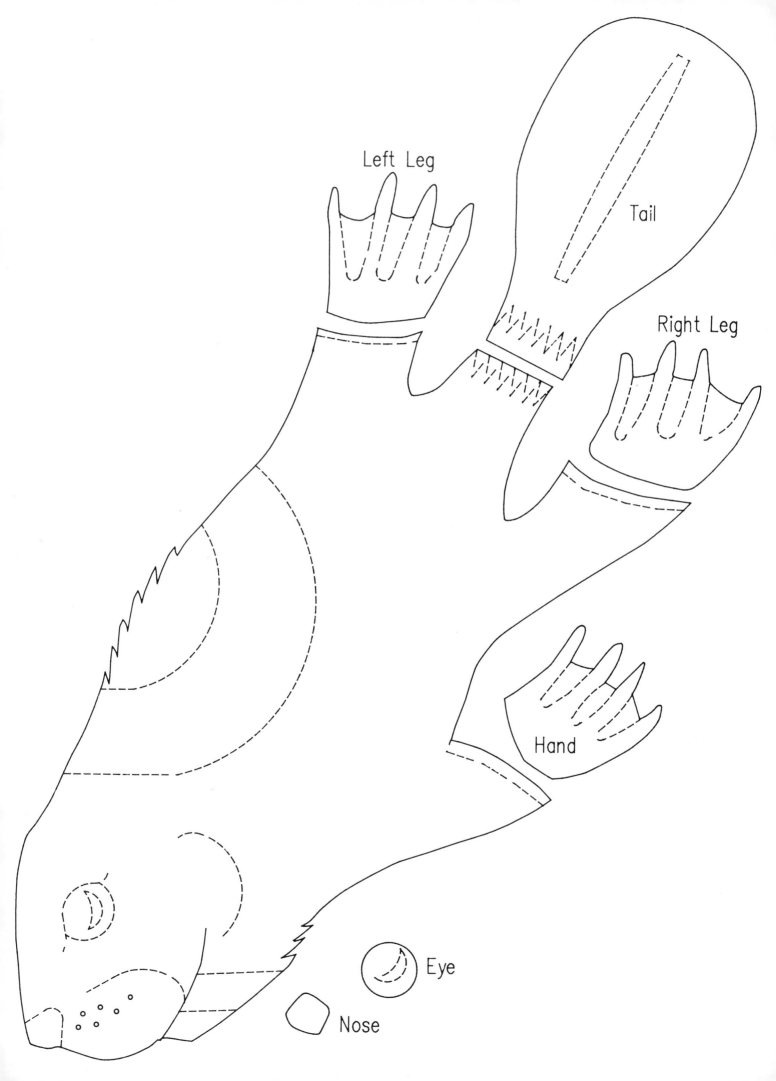

Left Leg

Tail

Right Leg

Hand

Eye

Nose

Tail Spine

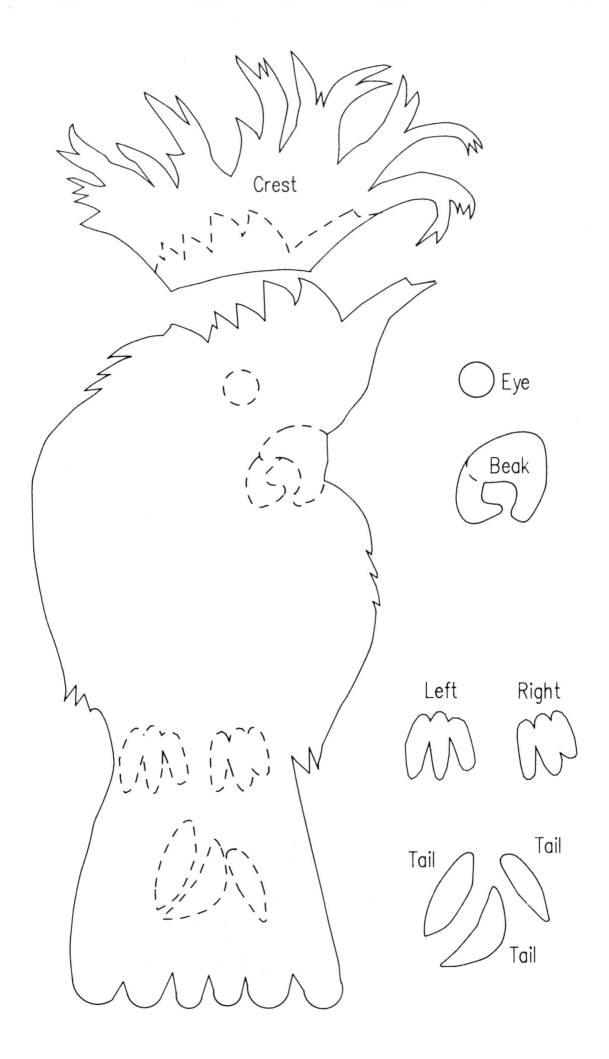

Crest

Eye

Beak

Left   Right

Tail   Tail

Tail

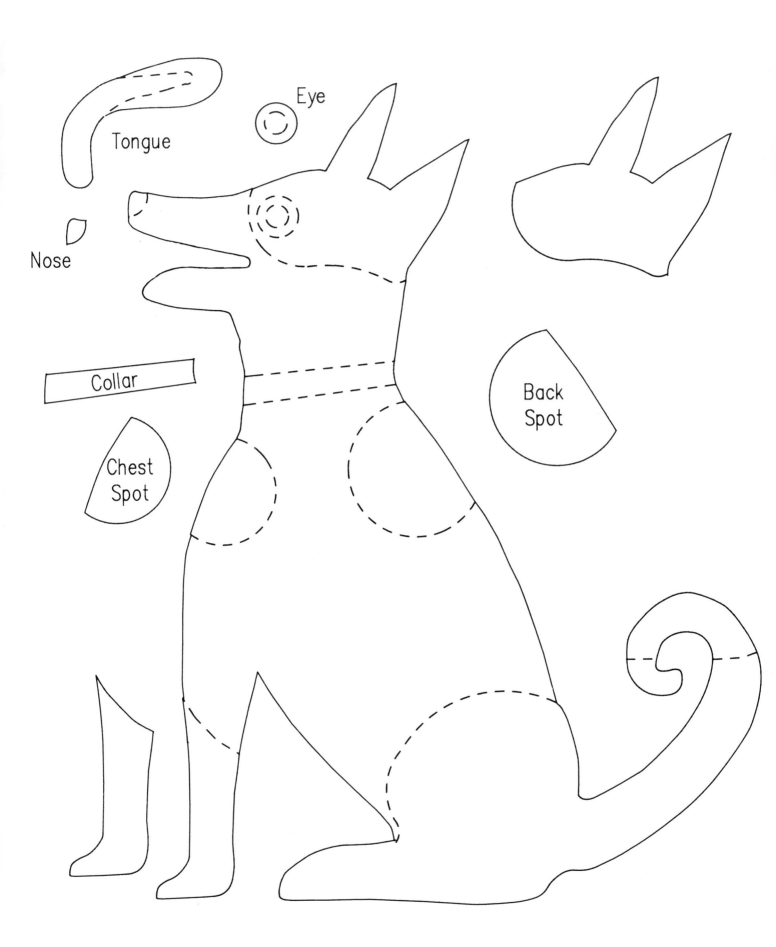

Tongue

Eye

Nose

Collar

Chest
Spot

Back
Spot

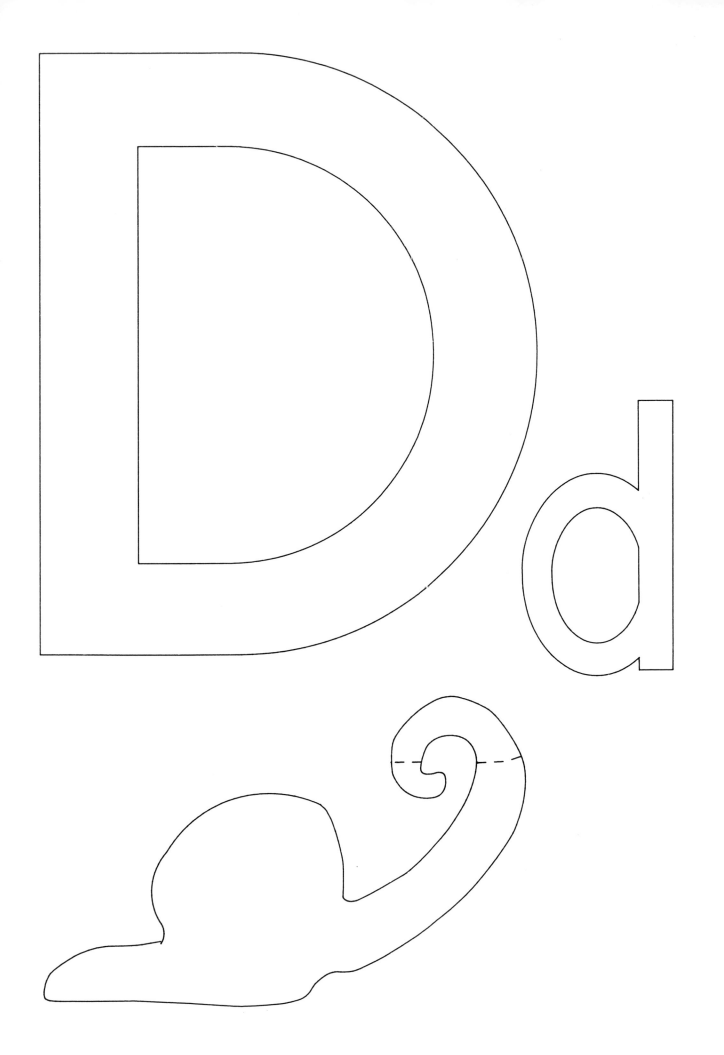

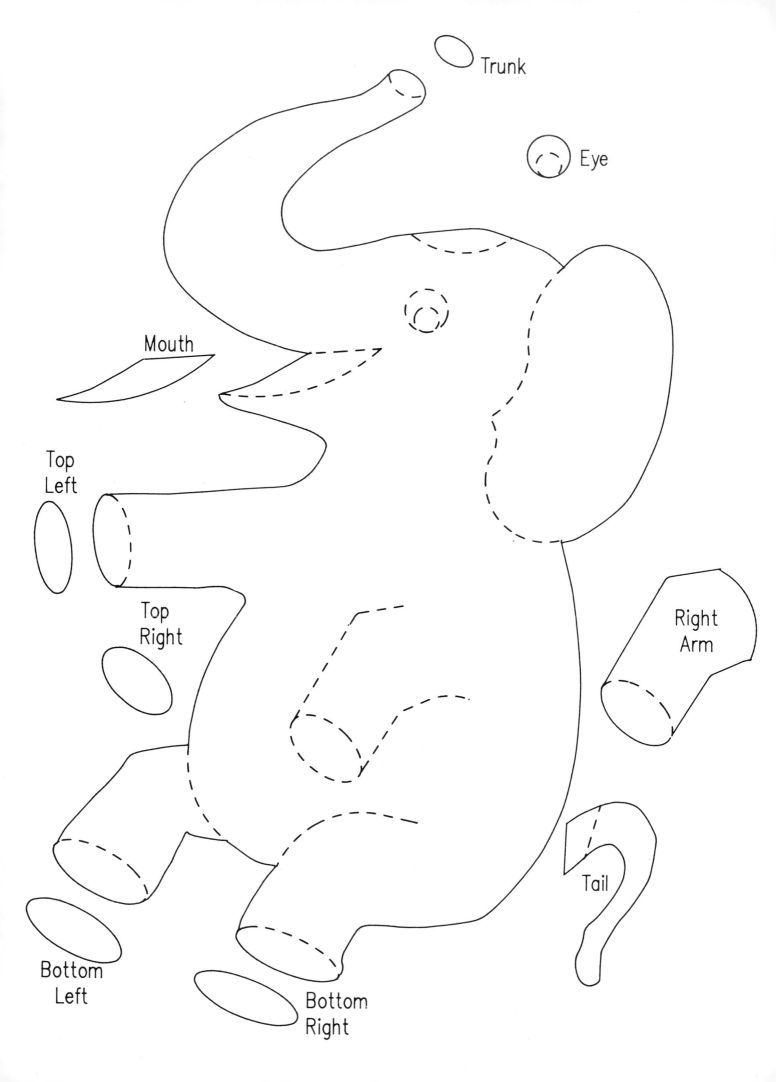

Trunk

Eye

Mouth

Top
Left

Top
Right

Right
Arm

Bottom
Left

Bottom
Right

Tail

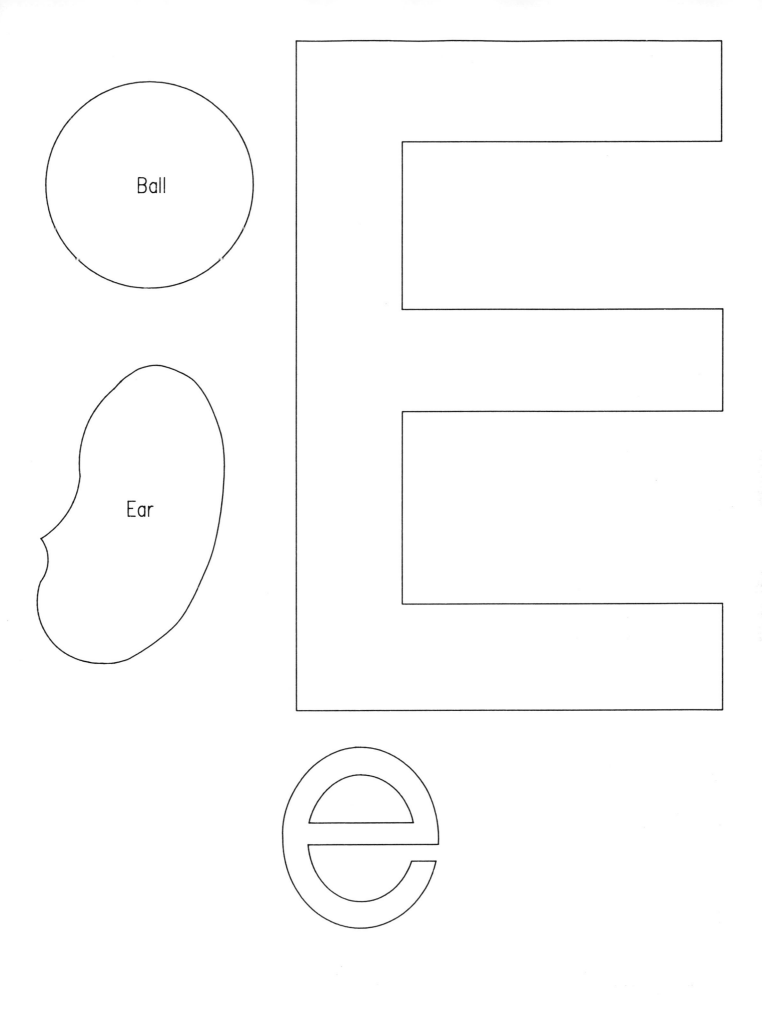

Ball

Ear

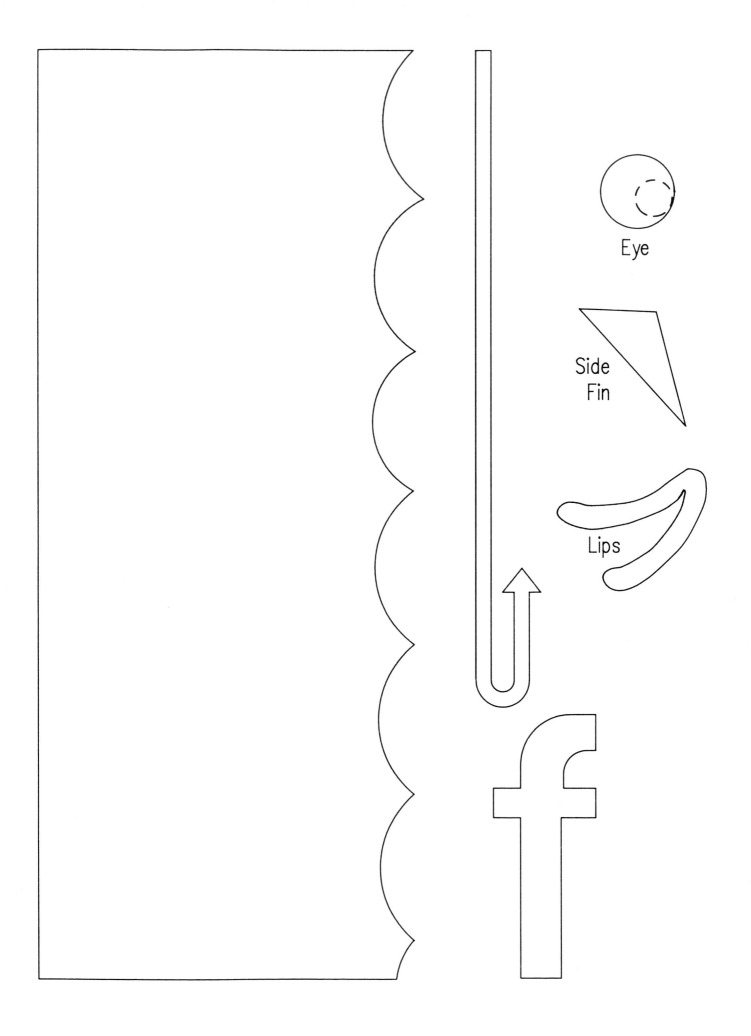

Eye

Side
Fin

Lips

f

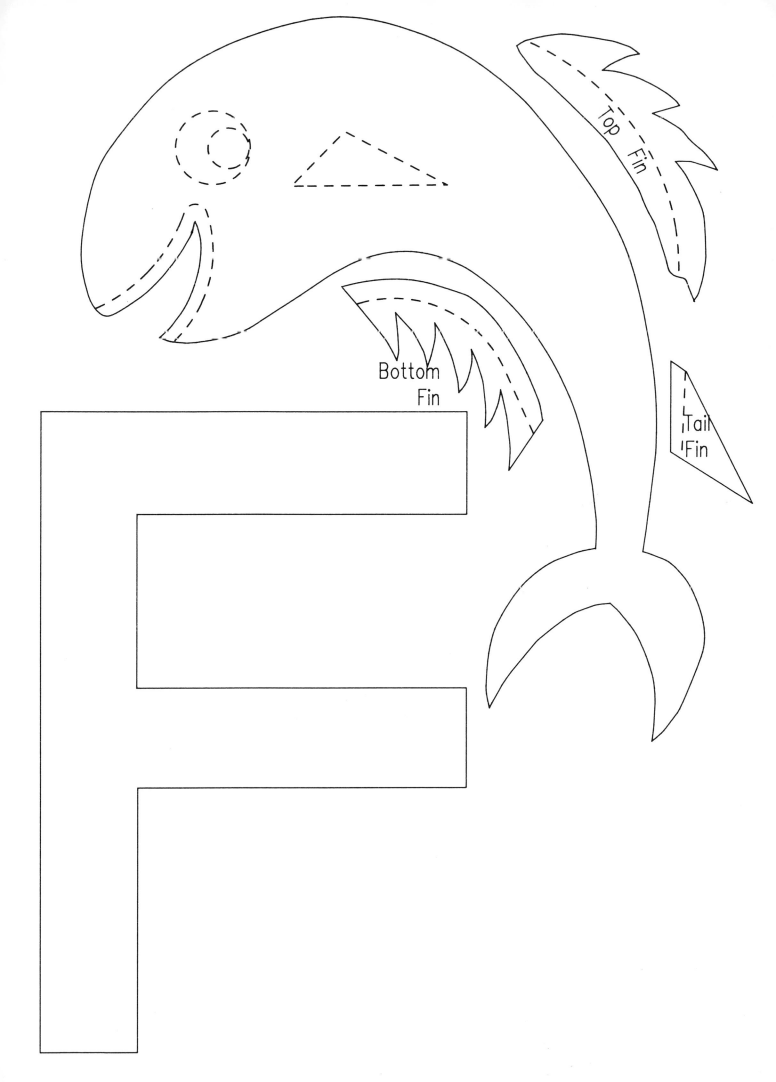

Top Fin

Bottom
Fin

Tail
Fin

Egg

Beak

g

Eye

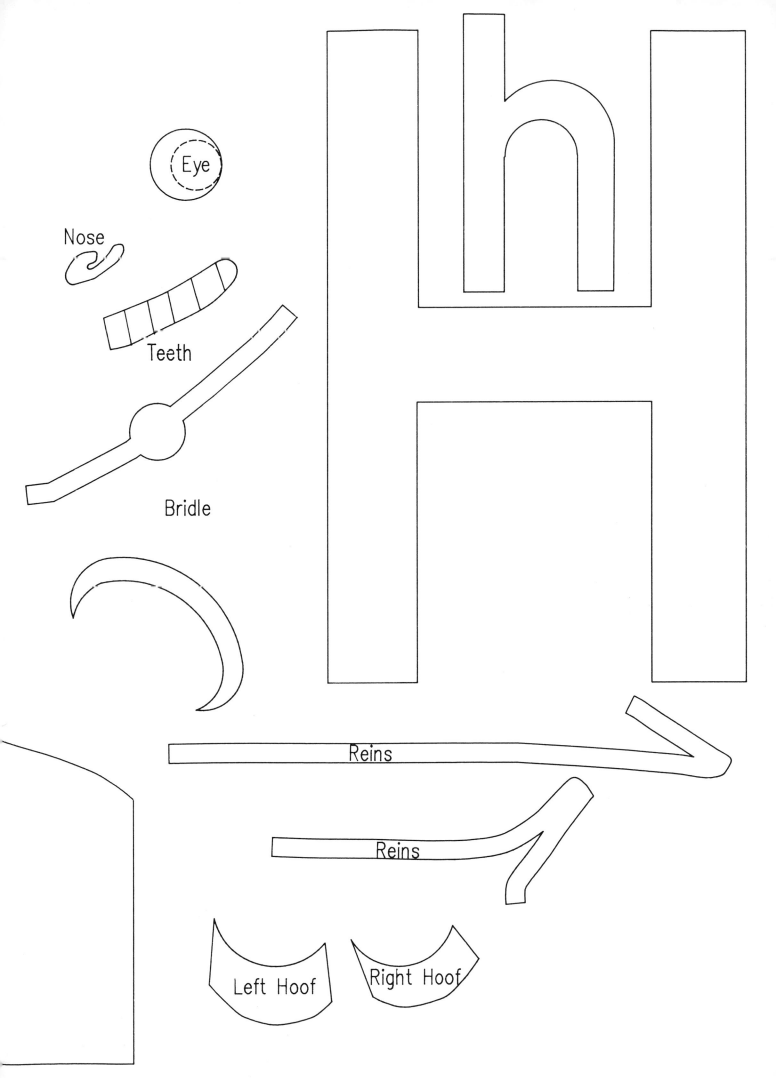

Eye

Nose

Teeth

Bridle

Reins

Reins

Left Hoof

Right Hoof

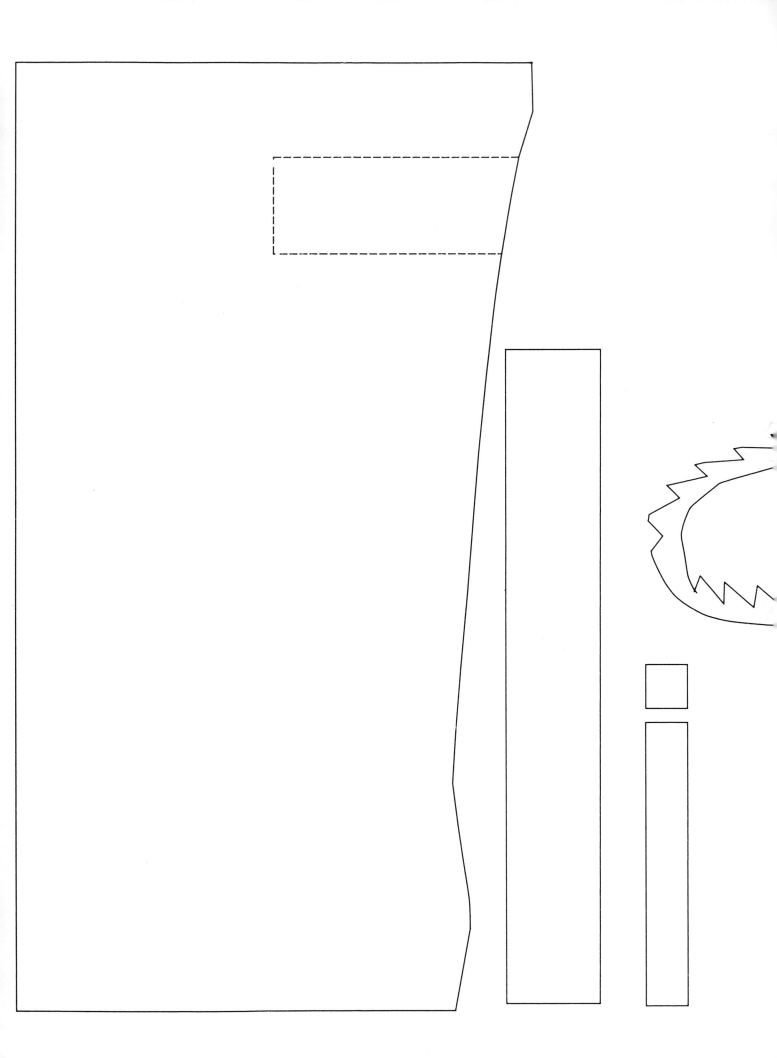

Mouth

Eye

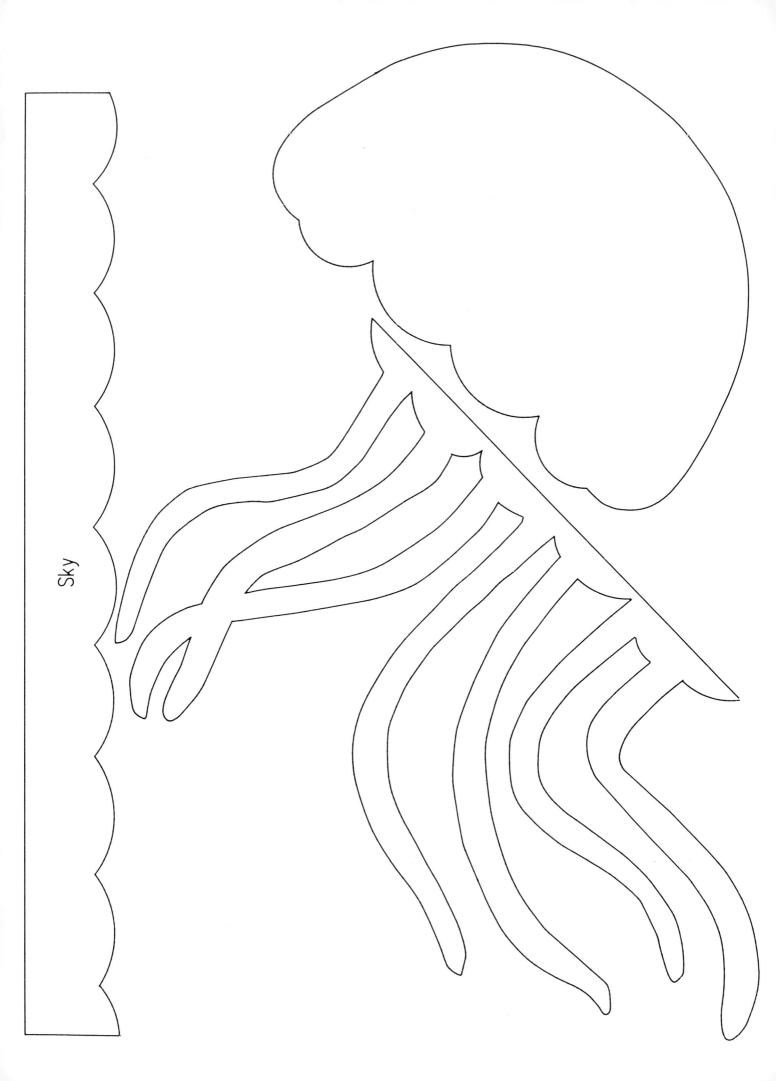

Sky

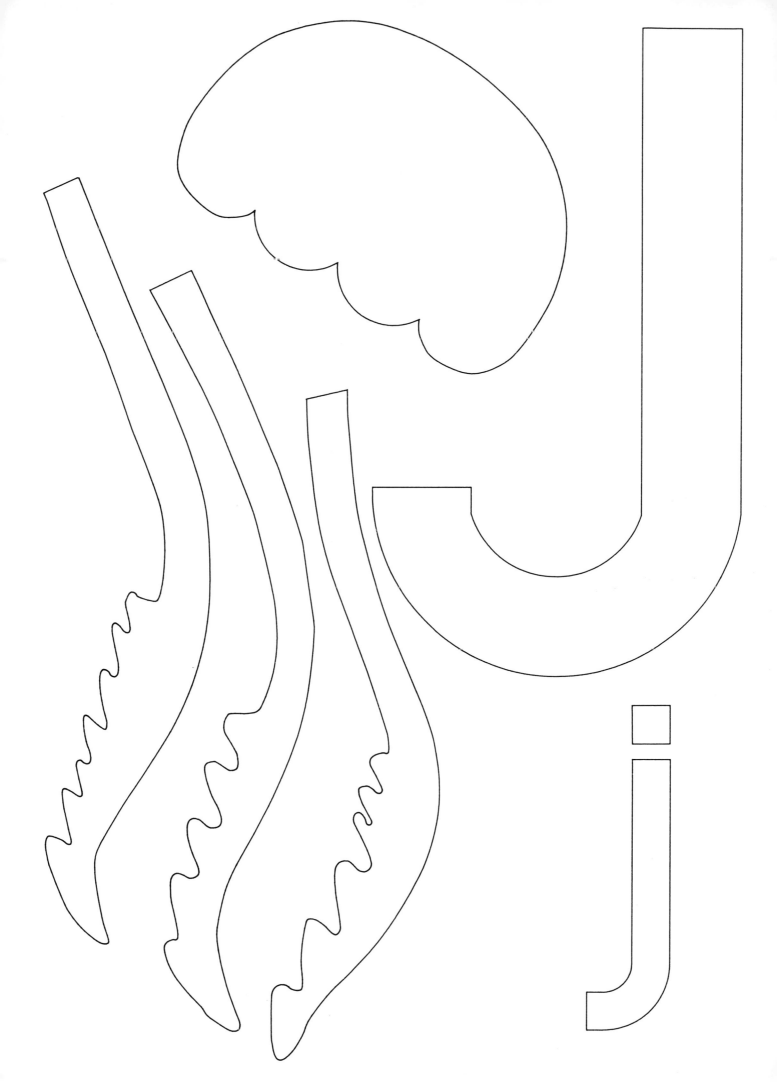

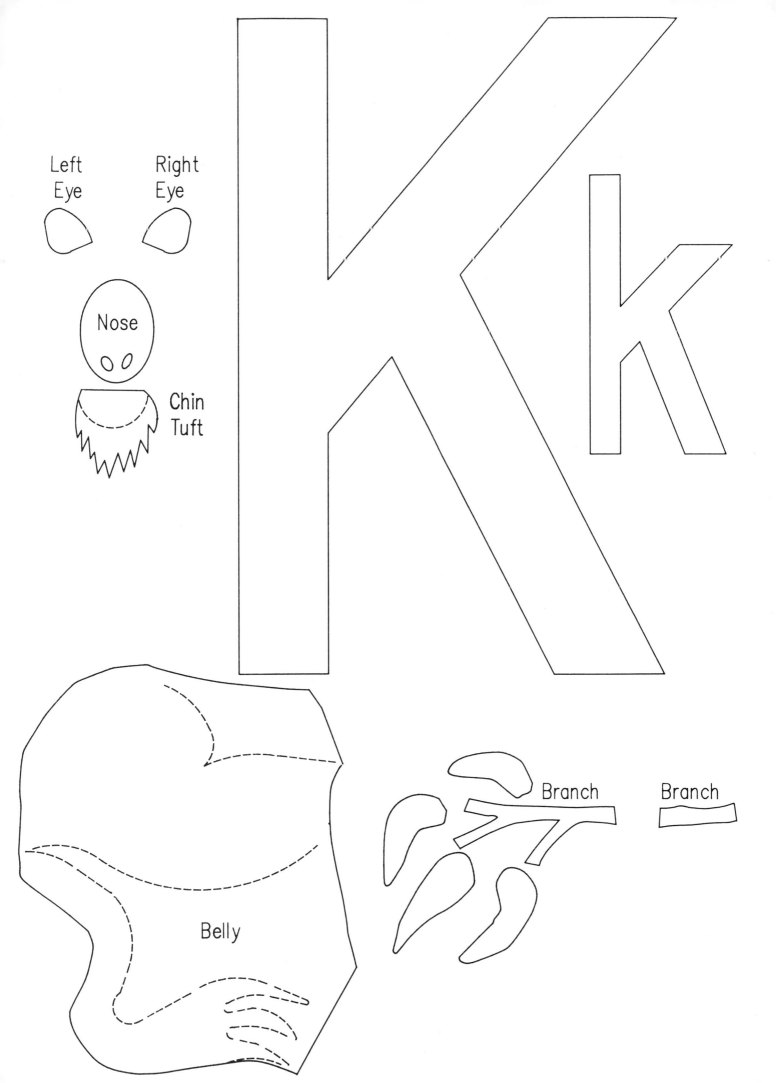

Left
Eye

Right
Eye

Nose

Chin
Tuft

K k

Belly

Branch   Branch

Tail
Tuft

Ear

Ear

Left
Eye

Right
Eye

Chin

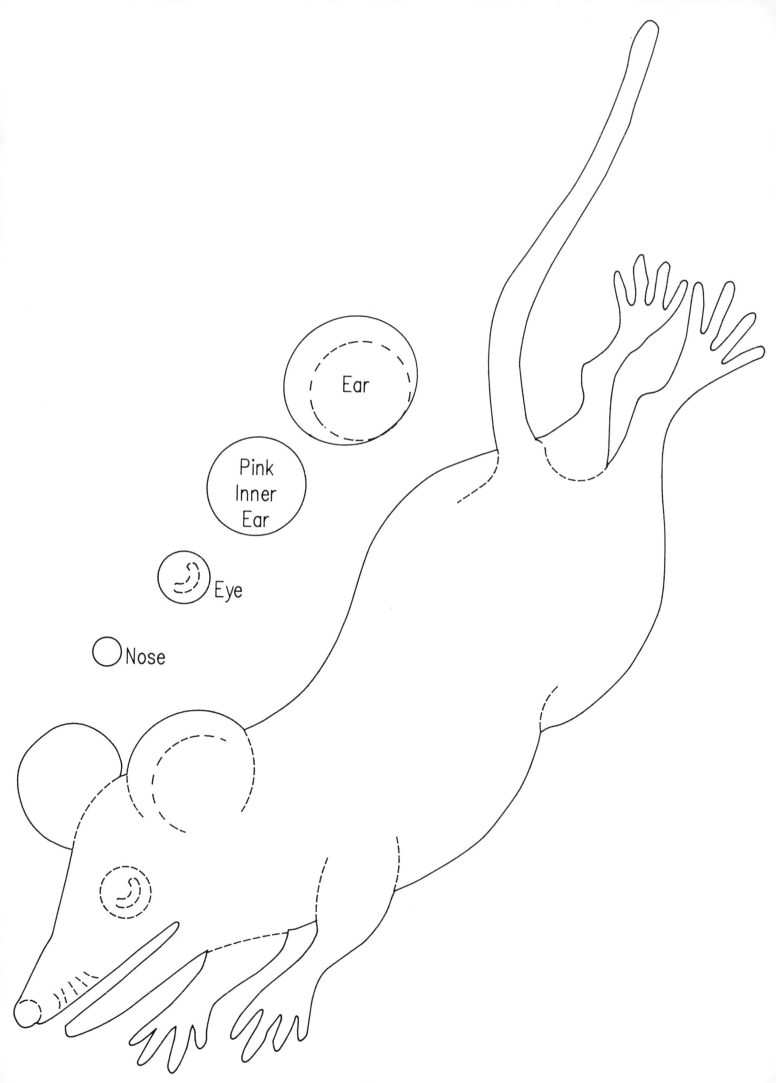

Ear

Pink
Inner
Ear

Eye

Nose

Nest (front)

Chick

Beak

Nest background

N

n

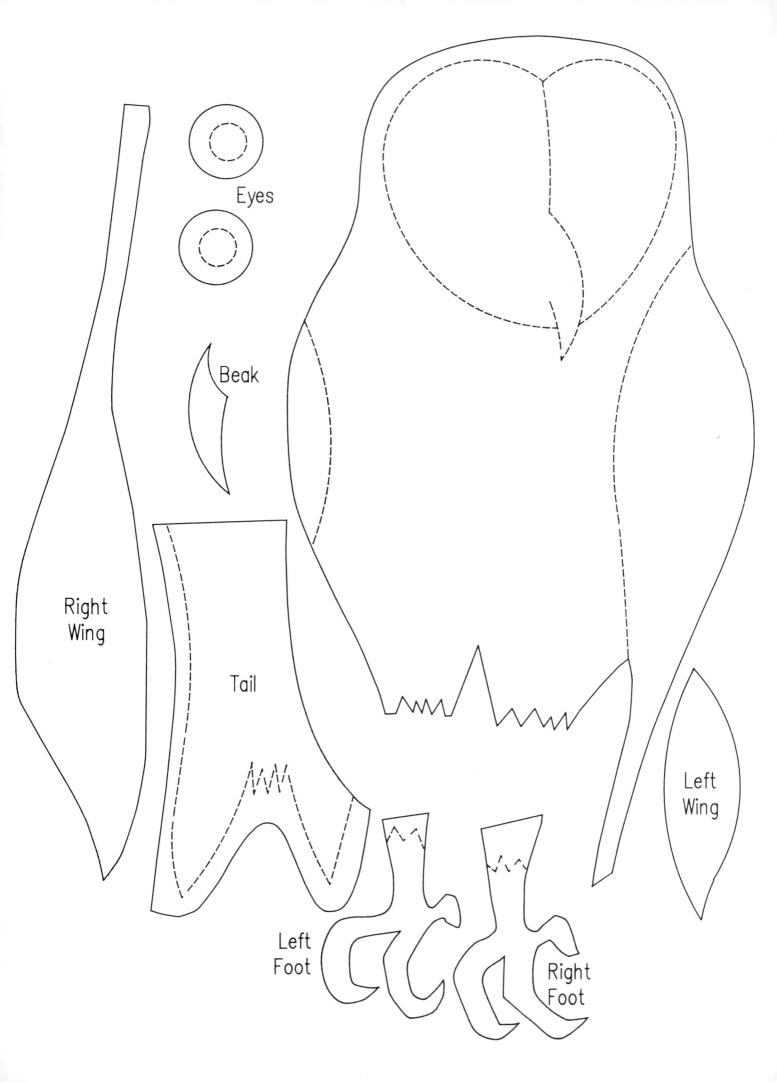

Eyes

Beak

Right
Wing

Tail

Left
Wing

Left
Foot

Right
Foot

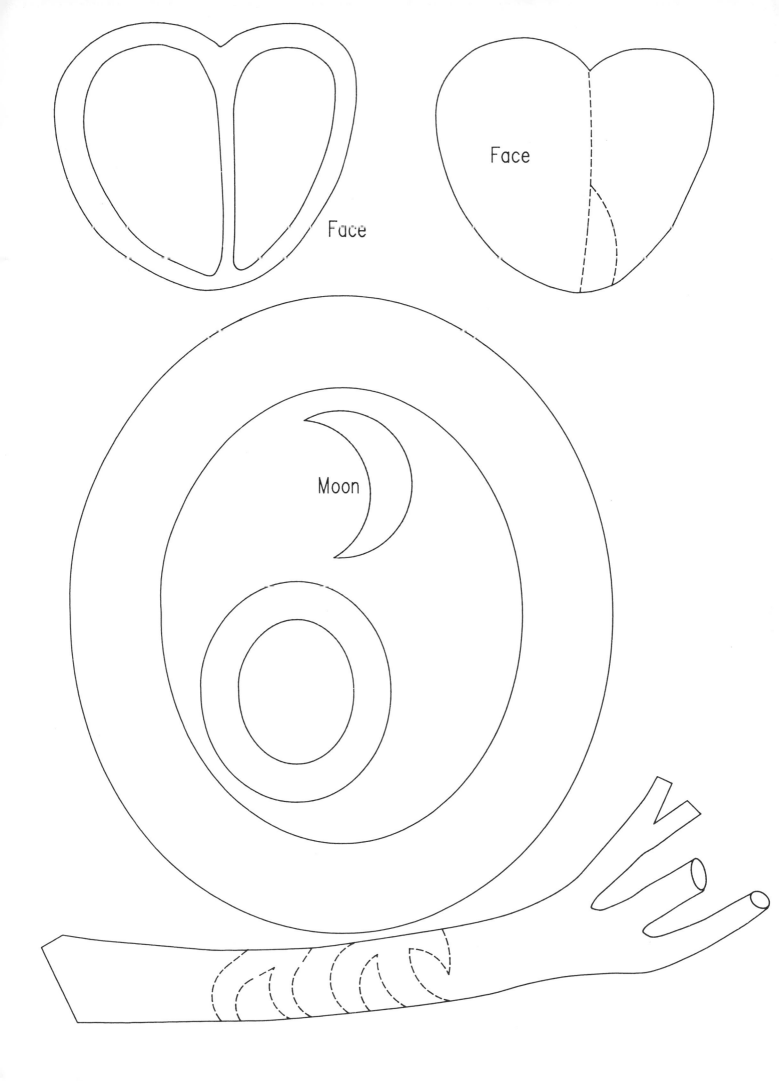

Face

Face

Moon

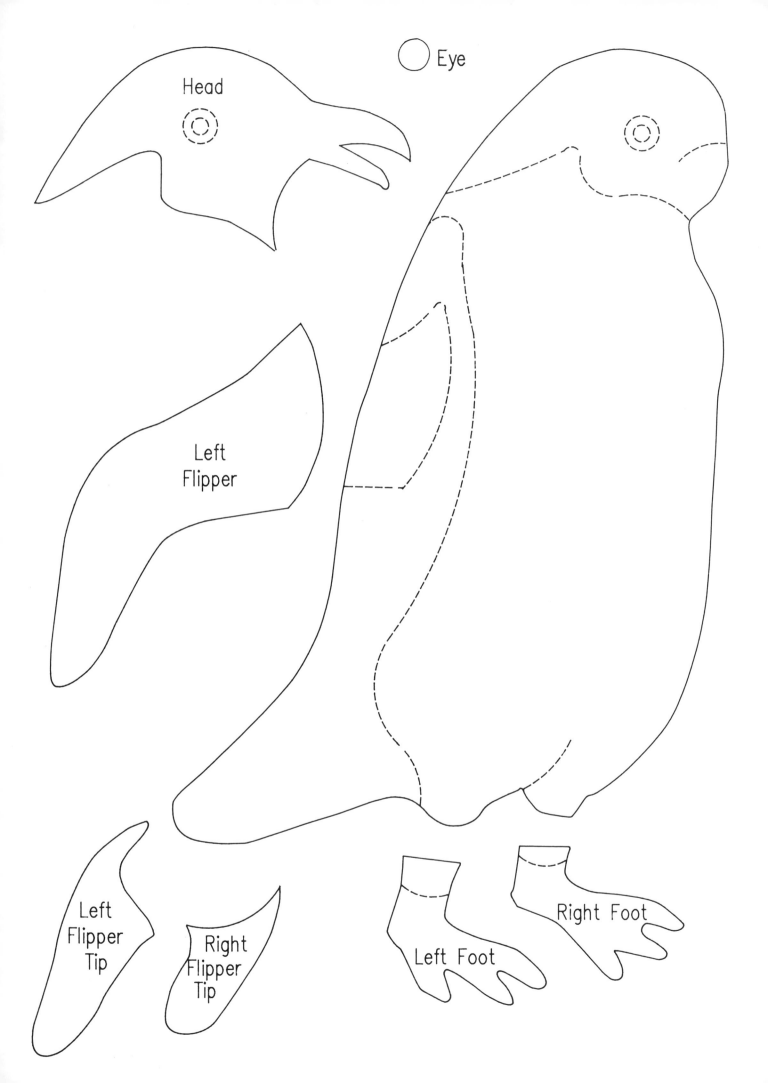

Head

Eye

Left
Flipper

Left
Flipper
Tip

Right
Flipper
Tip

Left Foot

Right Foot

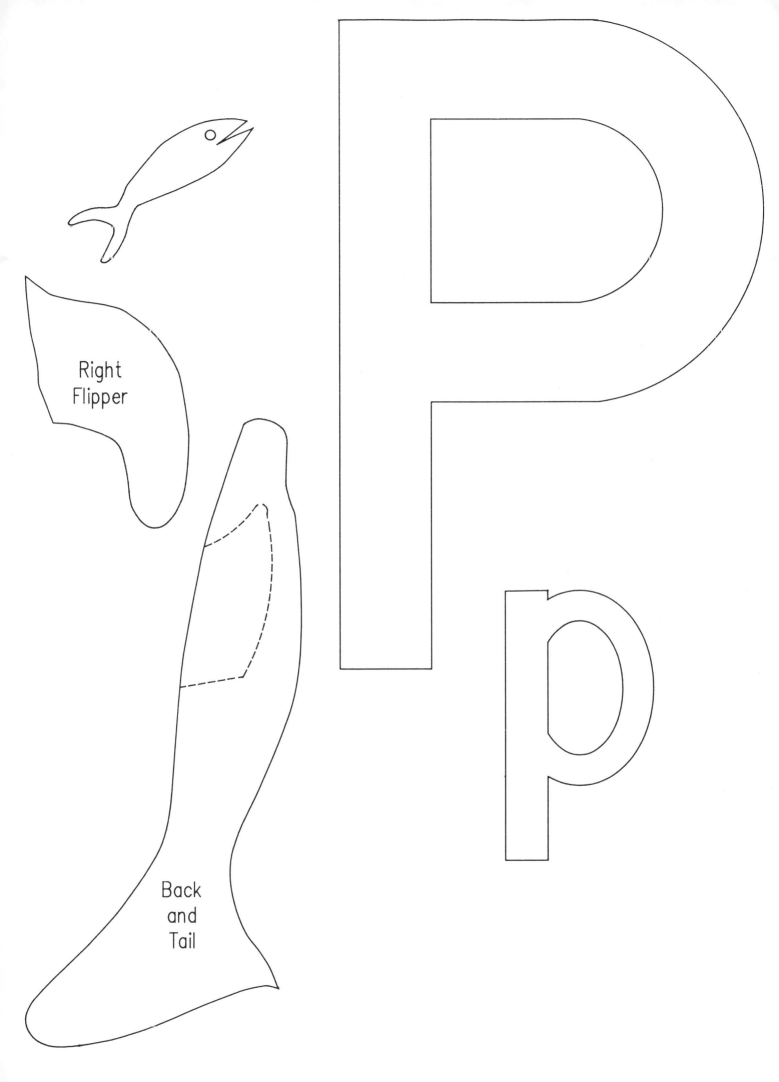

Right
Flipper

Back
and
Tail

P

p

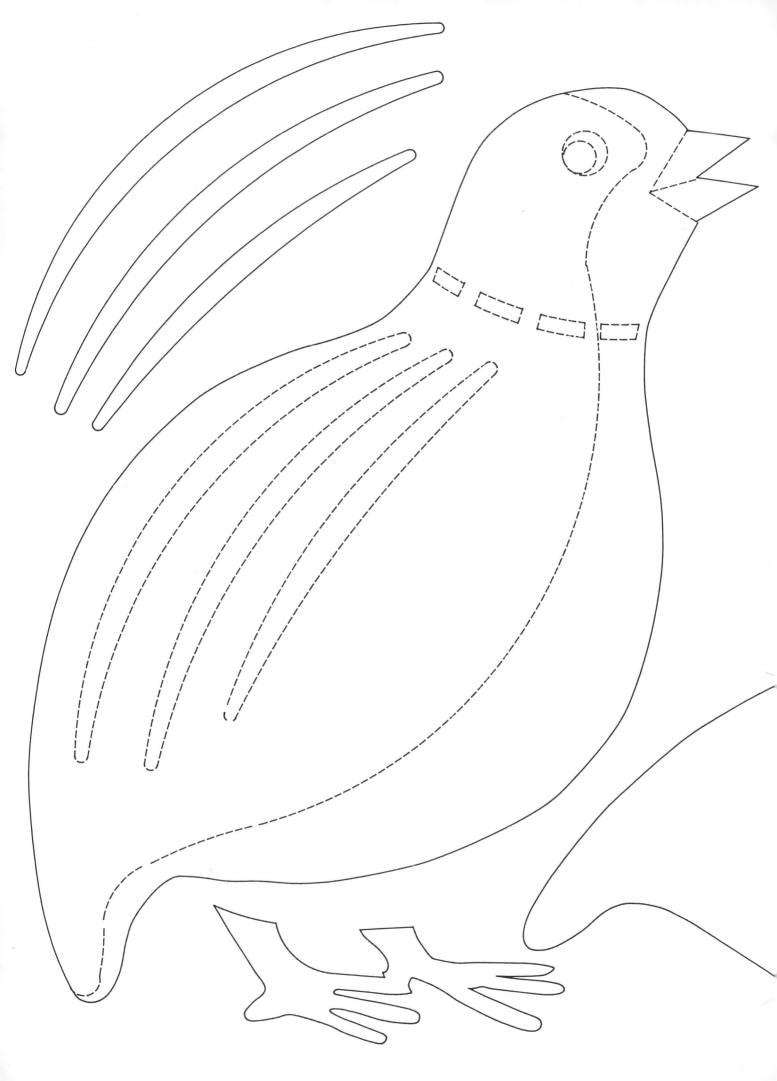

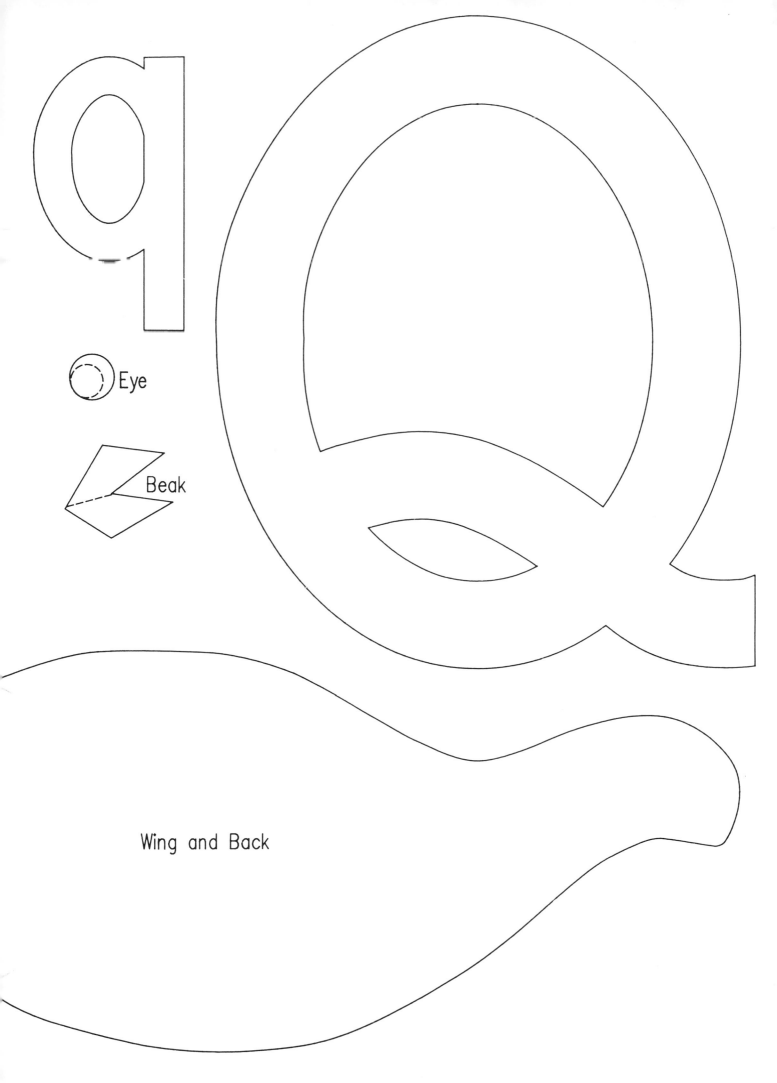

q

Eye

Beak

Wing and Back

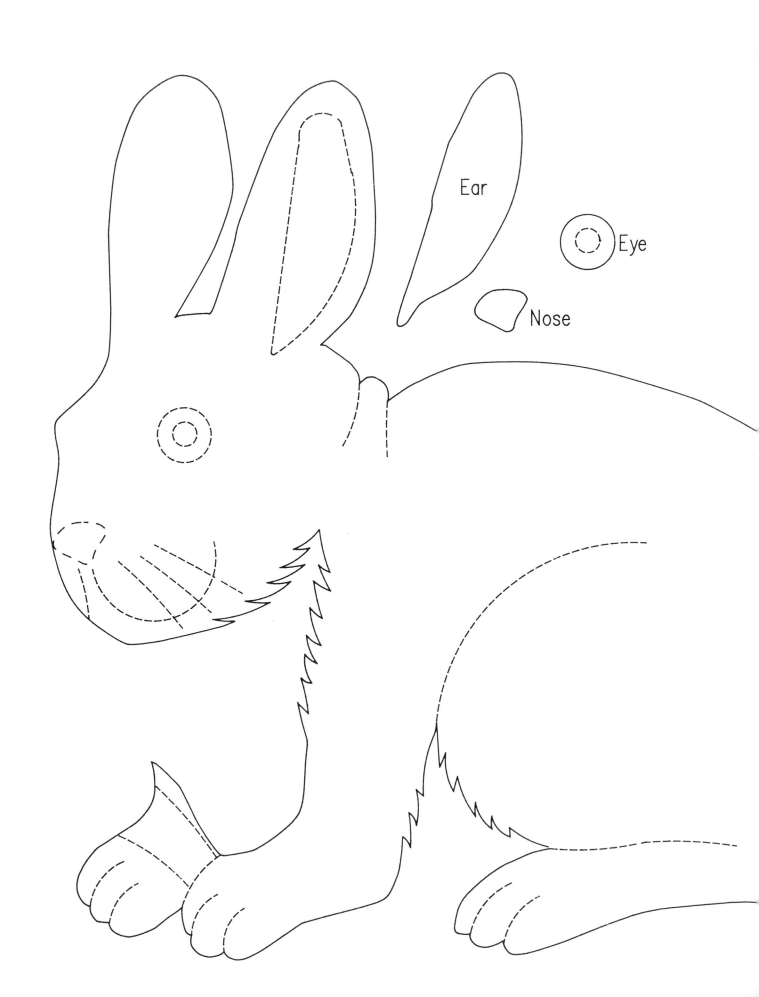

Ear

Eye

Nose

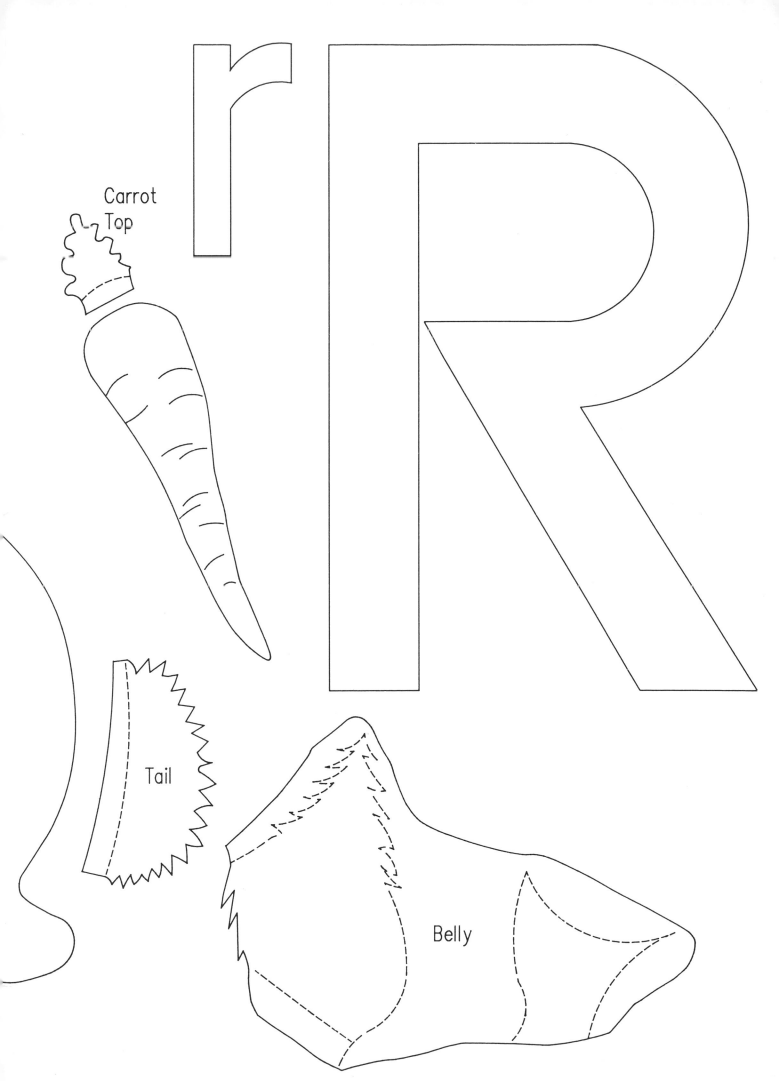

r R

Carrot Top

Tail

Belly

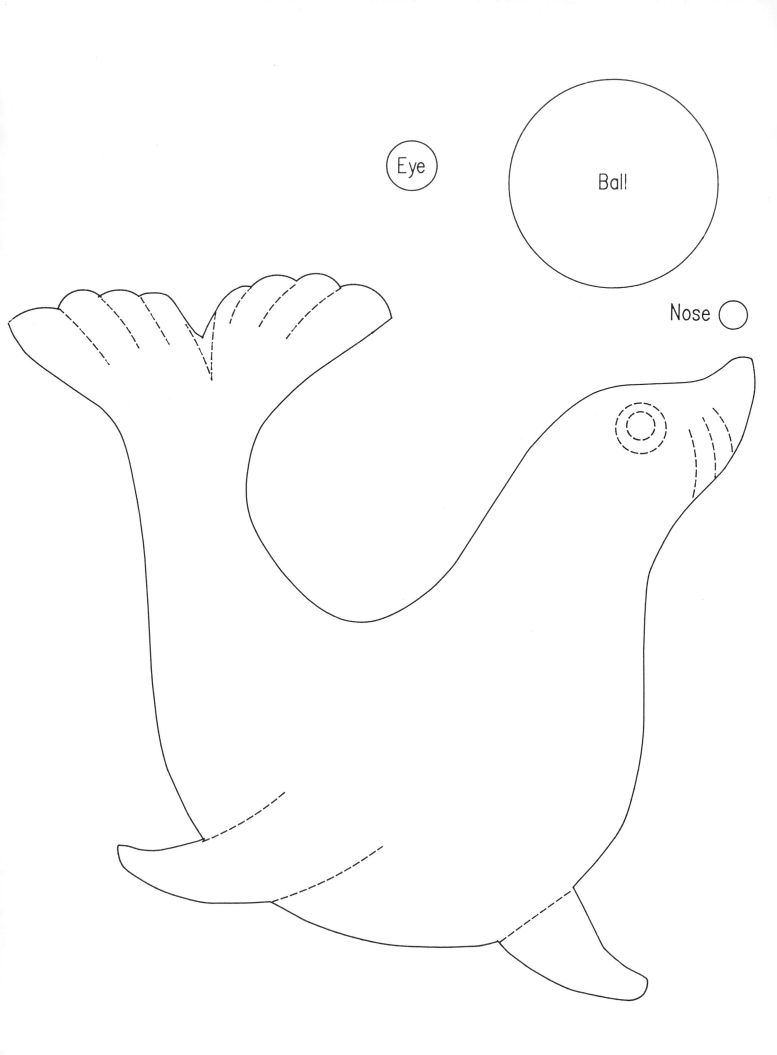

Eye

Ball

Nose

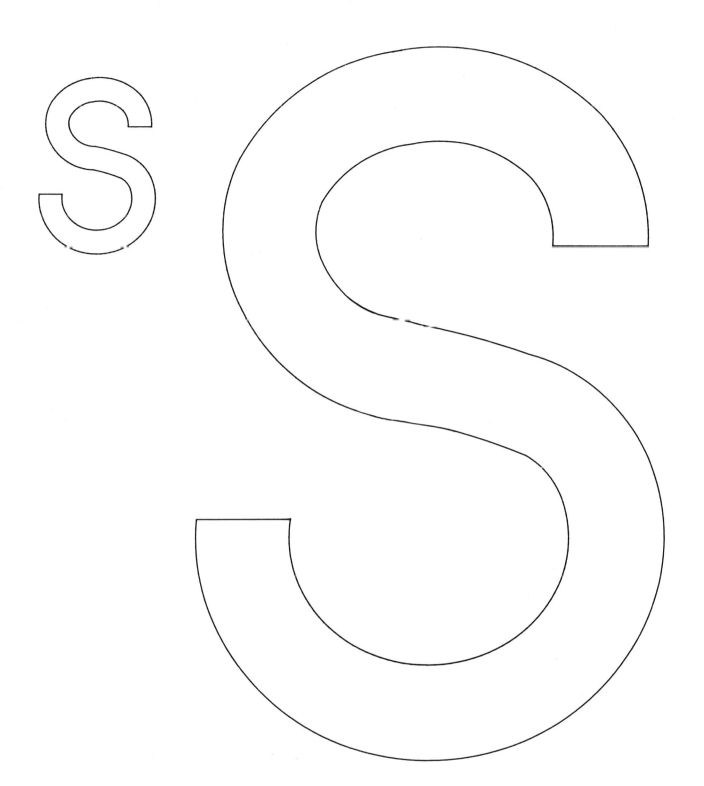

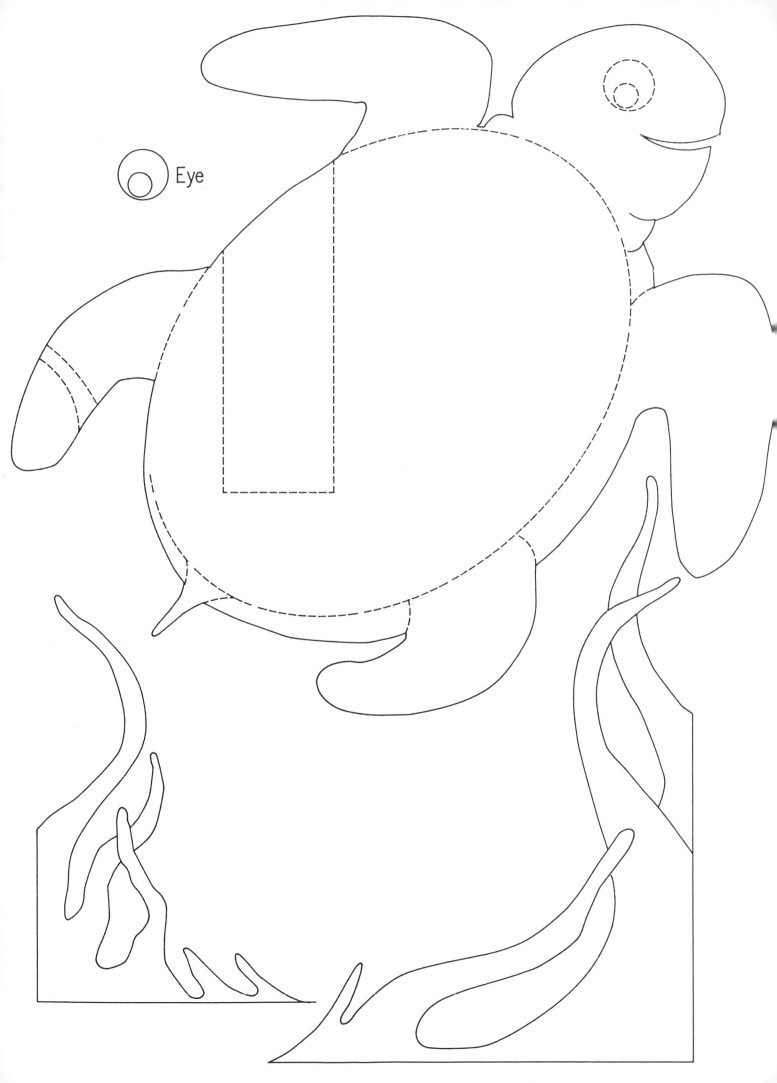

Eye

Back

Ear

Eye

Nose

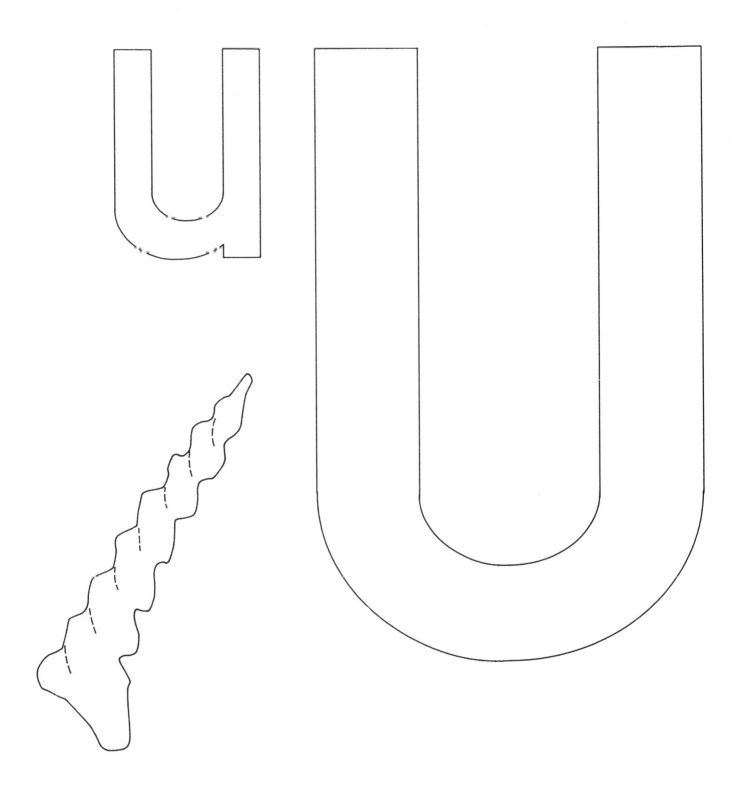

Grass

Wing

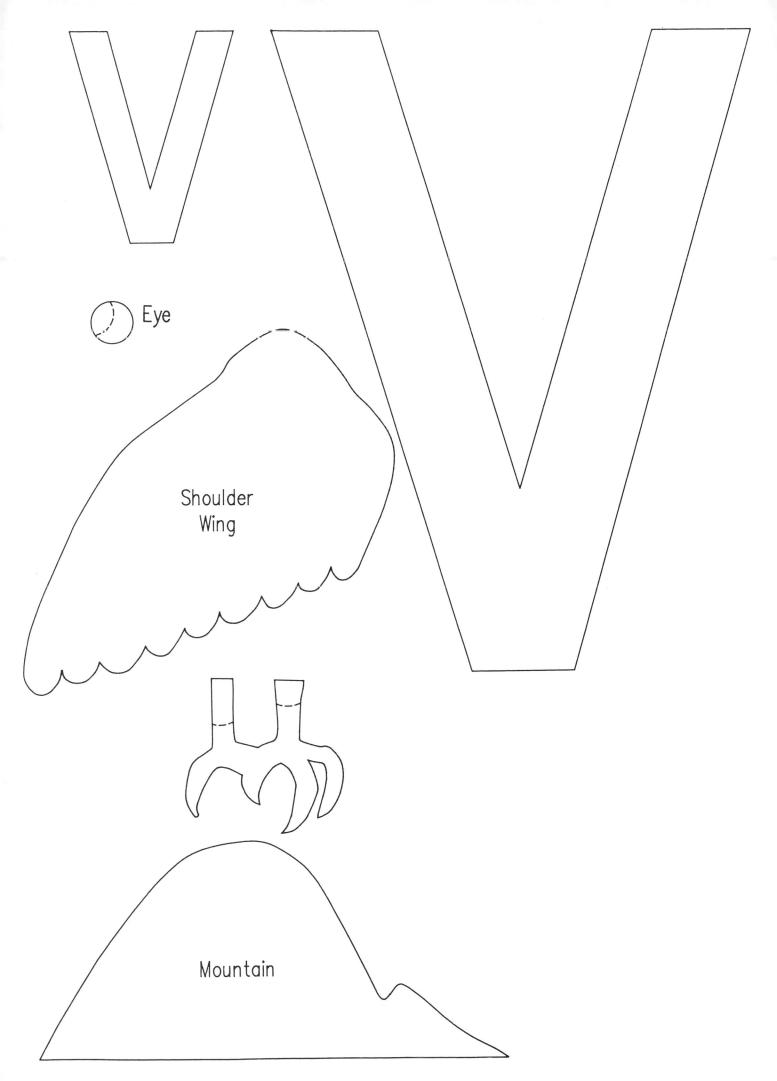

Eye

Shoulder
Wing

Mountain

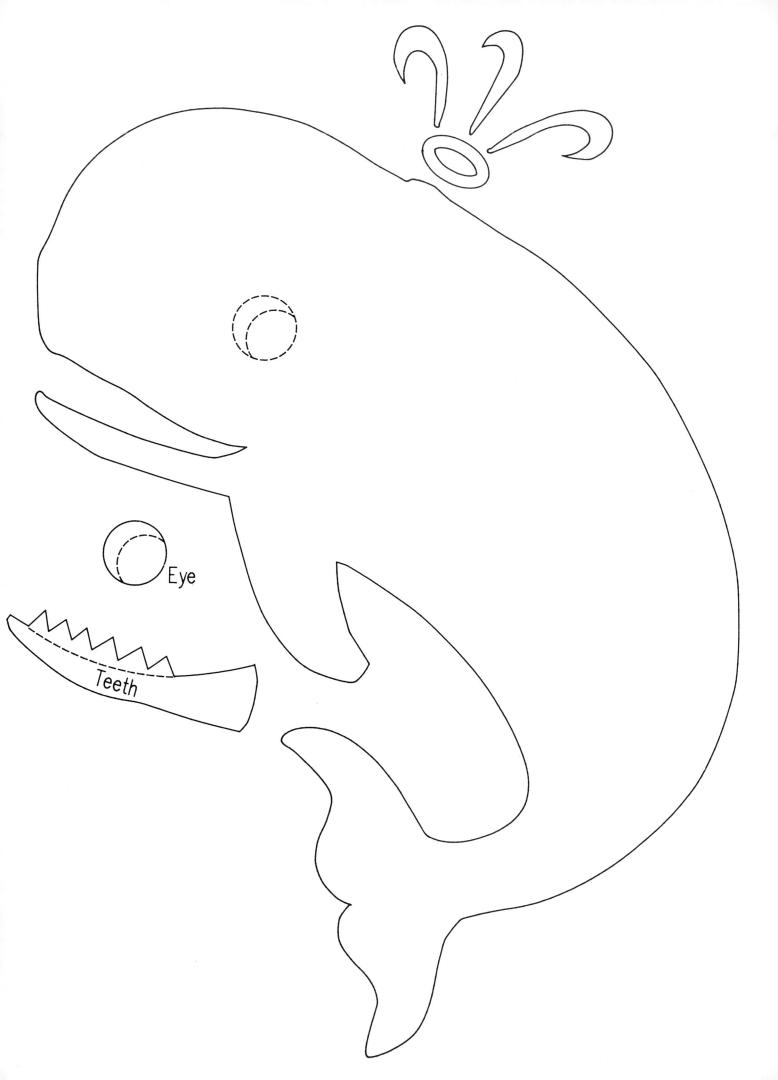

Eye

Teeth

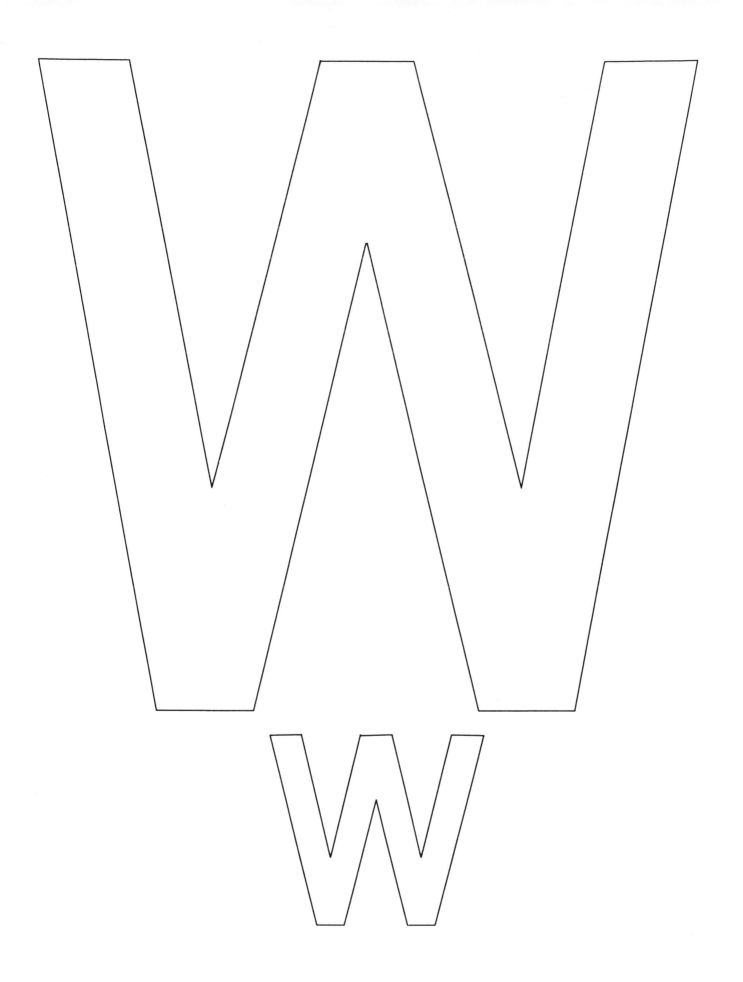

X X Eye Eye

Left Hand

L1 L2 L3

1 2 3 4 5 6

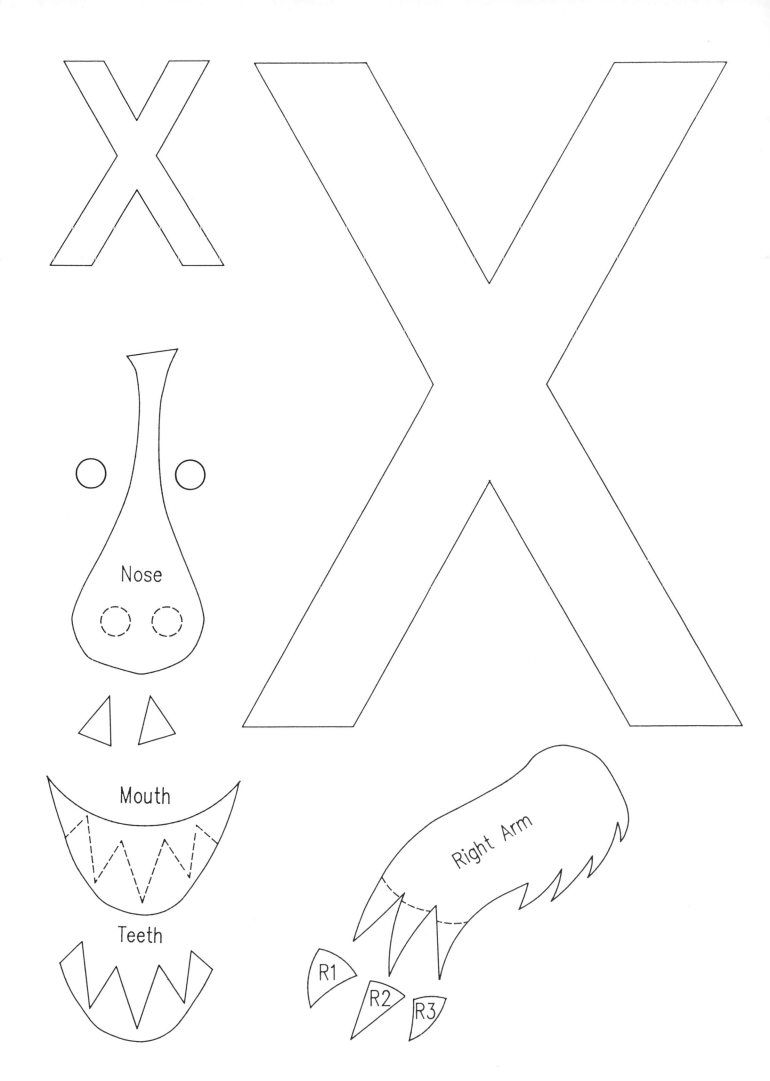

Nose

Mouth

Teeth

Right Arm

R1

R2

R3

Eye Eye

Eye Eye

Nose

Left
Front
Leg

Right
Front
Leg

Y

y

Mane

Left
Rear
Leg

Right
Rear
Leg

Ear

Neck 3

Neck 2

Neck 1

8

9

7

6

Grass

5

4

3

2

1

Tail

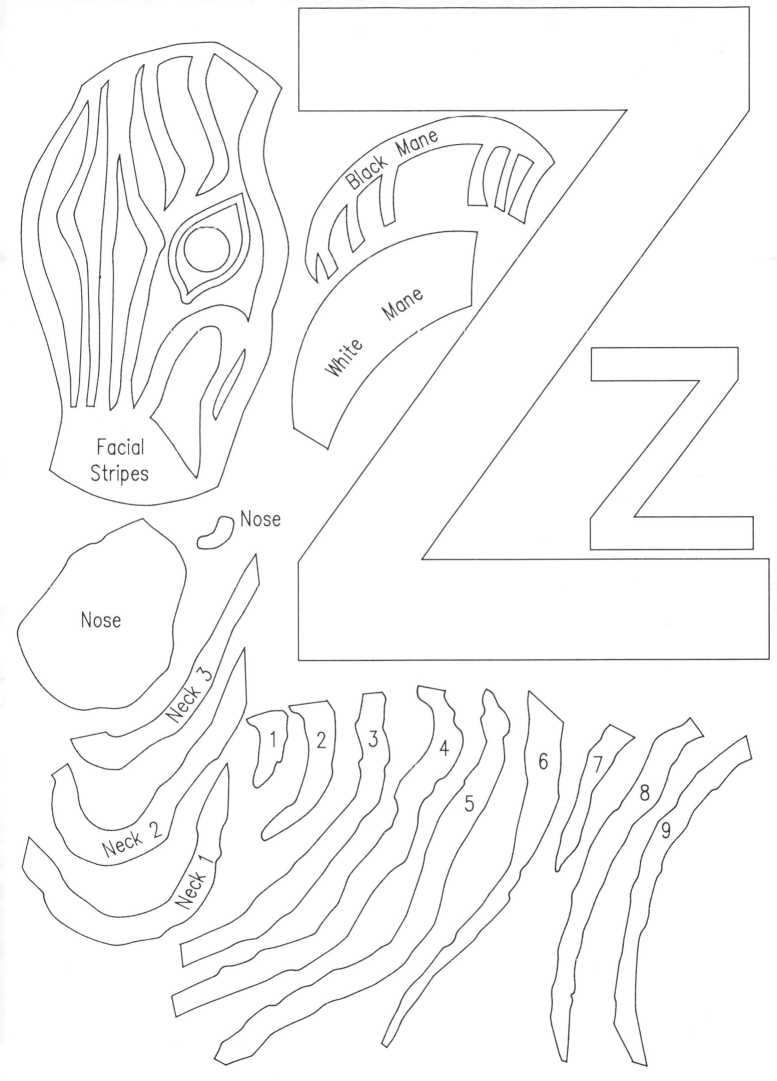

Facial
Stripes

Black Mane

White Mane

Nose

Nose

Neck 3

Neck 2

Neck 1

1

2

3

4

5

6

7

8

9

Z z